Having A Bad Hair Day

Clare C Davison

This book is dedicated to George, who passed away from cancer in 2014. He never saw the final draft.

To Hilary, who passed away from cancer in 2016, for being my strength, support and my honest friend.

You are both missed very much.

Chapters

CHAPTER 1 – NOT-SO-NORMAL LIFE.....................................1

CHAPTER 2 – I'VE FOUND A LUMP 10

CHAPTER 3 – GETTING MY BITS CHECKED......................17

CHAPTER 4 – THIS WAS NOT IN MY LIFE PLAN 25

CHAPTER 5 – HANGING BY A THREAD 36

CHAPTER 6 – IT'S ALL GONE TITS UP!..............................43

CHAPTER 7 – SQUATTERS' RIGHTS! 50

CHAPTER 8 – OPERATION CLARE.....................................58

CHAPTER 9 – ANGEL IN SCRUBS 66

CHAPTER 10 – TIT FOR TAT 74

CHAPTER 11 – RECOVERY MODE 79

CHAPTER 12 – THE RINSE CYCLE.....................................87

CHAPTER 13 – HAIR TODAY, GONE TOMORROW...........94

CHAPTER 14 – MILK AND MAKE UP.................................102

CHAPTER 15 – KEEP IT UNDER YOUR HAT 111

CHAPTER 16 – BALD AND BRAVE....................................120

CHAPTER 17 – WITH OR WITHOUT YOU.........................135

CHAPTER 18 – HERO IN SCRUBS 143

CHAPTER 19 – THE FINAL EVICTION 154

CHAPTER 20 – THE HEAT IS ON 163

CHAPTER 21 – KNIGHT OF ONCOLOGY 173

CHAPTER 22 – GETTING IT OFF MY CHEST 181

CHAPTER 23 – UNEXPECTED LOSSES 189

CHAPTER 24 – PLEASE LOOK AFTER "BEAR", THANK
YOU 194

CHAPTER 25 – I'M BULLET PROOF 207

EPILOGUE – TOM'S VERDICT 221

MY ONGOING AFTER EFFECTS FROM CANCER 223

THANK YOU IS NEVER ENOUGH 225

CHAPTER 1 – NOT-SO- NORMAL LIFE

Someone once said to me that if it wasn't for bad luck, you wouldn't have any luck. Never has a truer word been said. Let me tell you about the past 45 years, as I am typing with fingers crossed that the next 45 years have room for vast improvement!

I was born in Glasgow in 1969 to my Scottish father and my half-English, half-Irish mother. And I wonder why I am so confused! We moved back to my mother's home town in Hinckley, Leicestershire when I was six weeks old and remained there. My parents' relationship had broken down and we were moving in with my step-grandmother and maternal grandfather.

He sadly passed away before I was a year old. My parents had moved back and forth from Hinckley to Glasgow with my two older sisters, Tracey and Sarah, where there is an age gap of almost four years between all three of us. Two years later my dad moved back in with us from Scotland and we were all back together.

We spent a lot of weekends and school holidays back in Glasgow where my father's family lived. It was great and exciting to go back to visit and play in a different community. The ice cream vans seemed to sell everything. I loved all the Scottish treats and a roll with square sausage, which made my visits back to Glasgow more exciting.

My father was the twentieth of 21 children so there was always plenty of family to visit. Putting a family tree together always seemed an unsuccessful challenge, but one of my cousins has now successfully progressed with it more than I could. Aunties and uncles would come down to visit us. They remained close as they had practically raised my father and were very involved in our lives. Sadly, over 20 years ago, our closest aunt was visiting us and passed away at our home on New Year's morning from a heart attack. She was more like a natural parent to us than an aunt and her passing was a huge connection we were to lose with Scotland.

I have always been a great animal lover, but I was attacked and hospitalised by my aunt's dog at age 4 and nearly blinded in my left eye, of which I still bear the scars. Despite my recovery it changed my contact with dogs, although my love for them remained. Cats are my domain!

I attended catholic schools and had a pretty good education if I am honest, but by the age of 15 I was ready to leave school. It was at this age I lost my step-grandmother. I was with her when she passed at home and was devastated by her loss. When she was 18, she had been engaged to a local boy but her family did not approve and sent her away to live with family in America. Sadly, during this journey, the ship that she sailed on received an S.O.S from the Titanic. They were too far away and could not assist. I have her engagement ring from this sad memory.

In later years she met my grandfather who had been widowed on the birth of his fifth daughter, my mum. Two of his daughters had already passed as children and as he ran his coal merchant business and raised a family, my mum was cared for by a family friend. As he was preparing to go to war, he and my step-grandmother decided to marry to keep the family together. He did not have to go to war, being Irish, but he believed as he had three English daughters he would fight for them.

I had lost all interest in education and had found hair dye, modelling, cigarettes, alcohol and other recreational past-times. My parents gave me the choice to stay in education or get a job, so I left school. Within two weeks I was working in a local record shop on the Youth Training Scheme (YTS). I was almost 16 years old and this was a job I adored. For £40 per week and in full time employment I did jobs there that would make your teeth curl!

At school, I had been interested in typing and office practice, so when I turned 18, I decided to move onto a different career path. I think by this stage I had only received a £5 rise so I was not exactly flushed with cash. Office and factory work were paying more and some of my friends would be on three times my income, so I moved into temporary office work through agencies and found my forte. From the majority of temporary roles I took on, I would be offered permanent work, but they were always out of town or in difficult areas of Leicester to get to, and I could not drive. I couldn't afford to drive!

Regular work became a hit and miss with the agencies so I took

—

a local job working for an aromatherapy company in charge of the orders in the warehouse. The smells from the premises were absolutely divine, and resulted in us smelling just as good! I met some great friends there and in October 1988 I had met my first serious boyfriend. He was three years older than me and a friend's brother. He worked as a knitting machine mechanic. Factories in the town were at their peak back then although there is barely one left now. He had a two year old daughter whom I happily accepted as part of our relationship and who in later years has become part of our lives now. In April 1990, after a lovely meal, he got down on bended knee and proposed.

In order to save for a new home, I took the position as a secretary at a knitwear company. Six months later the accounts office lady was leaving and after three days of training, my job developed into bookkeeping. To supplement my slight rise in salary I modelled part-time for local clothes shops, hairdressers, charity shows, country shows, even at one point auditioning for the Clothes Show at the Pebble Mill Studios. Although it was a lot of fun I knew my future career did not lie there, but the extra income meant that we could afford to buy our own home in 1990. I was 22 years old when we married in 1992 and set about making plans for the future which would naturally include children at some point. I had always wanted children, possibly 3, but not as many as 21 like my paternal grandmother!

Within two years of being married our fortunes had changed. I had given up 'social' smoking as we were trying for a baby, we had moved to a larger home, and I was working in Leicester in a new bookkeeping role. On a cold January day, not long before leaving work and after feeling queasy for a couple of weeks, I felt particularly ill, and very sadly I lost our first baby. It was 11th January 1994, a date that is etched on my brain. I was not aware

—

at the time that I was pregnant and was sent home, in some pain and discomfort and naturally devastated. I spent the next few days resigned to the sofa with backache, painkillers and immense sadness.

However, within a month, I was back at the doctors with a positive pregnancy test. They were of the belief that I had been carrying twins and had lost one of them. Instead of being excited with the joy of knowing I was to become a mum, I felt devastated again. I was not sure if I could spend my life looking at one child knowing I should have had another one, plus feeling guilty that I should be happy one had survived, and was it going to survive? It did not also change the fact that I had still lost a child. I had to wait for a scan. Luckily this confirmed the baby was not a twin as I had only just become pregnant and the foetus was not yet three months old. My expected date was in November 1994, but within the week I was back at the doctors again. I had dreadful bouts of sickness, some lasting day and night, and with my pregnancy history I was immediately signed off from work. The sickness lasted for over six months and I presumed that I must be expecting a boy because he constantly played football inside me. I am an independent girl and as I am very house proud, at seven months pregnant I was re-grouting the fully tiled bathroom to occupy myself.

November arrived and so did a healthy boy, Thomas, after being induced 24 hours before. We were completely overwhelmed and we dressed him in a white baby grow and soft cap. He looked like a little cricketer and he was absolutely divine. This didn't stop him crying all night, so he was resigned to stay in the hospital nursery to avoid disturbing all the other babies. My middle sister Sarah and my mum came to visit us in the hospital, bringing a teddy bear larger than Thomas, who incidentally managed to cry all the way through the visit! Yelled actually! The next day I took him home and I was the proudest mum in the world. I still am.

Over the next two years, circumstances changed, as did the relationship with Thomas' father. I was 27 and he was 29 and he had changed his career. Looking back, I don't know if we married too young or if we could have changed things. I spent most of my days being mum and a housewife, whilst he spent most of his days and evenings at work and enjoying the company of other ladies. The inevitable happened when people grow apart and in 1997, after nearly five years of marriage, the decree absolute was granted. Thomas and I moved out of the family home, as I could not afford to keep it on my own. In many ways we were happy to leave behind the sad memories. Within a few weeks, I had lost my husband, his family, my son's father and our home.

This was to be a new start for Thomas and me. We moved into a rented home where we would live for two years, but with all this upheaval and the end of the marriage I had a bout of depression. We were then burgled and my car vandalised at this address, so nothing on the luck front had improved. It was not the best area of town to live in but we kept to ourselves. I was in a new relationship which sadly came to nothing.

With the help of family caring for Thomas, I returned to full time work to save enough money for a deposit to buy us a permanent home. This brought a time of great happiness and we had many happy memories in this home. Another relationship led to an engagement and a move to Nottingham for a fresh new start. Not surprisingly, this relationship failed, and after 18 months, Thomas and I moved back to Hinckley. During our time in Nottingham, my car was hit by a cement lorry. Luckily Thomas was not in the car as I was on my way to pick him up. From this accident I sustained an unaligned spine which you would not know to look at me. Despite a second bout of depression from the faltering relationship, I had made many good friends in Nottingham who supported me and Thomas. I remain good friends with all of these today, many have married and have become parents themselves now.

By 2006 I was in a new relationship with Darren. He was a year older than me. We had met at school, lost touch and had not seen each other for 23 years until we met again on a night out, exchanged numbers and began our relationship. He was going through a divorce with two daughters aged eight and ten who were welcomed into our family.

When Thomas, now known as Tom, reached 13 years old, his dad, who had remarried, decided to move permanently to Spain. Unfortunately, Tom learned of this decision via social media and was naturally devastated, not only by the decision, but the means of finding out. He had not been told personally. I can still clearly recall the day I picked him up off the floor after he had broken down. He had come downstairs and as I looked at him I asked him if he was OK.

"Not really," was his reply. I asked what was wrong. He had his back to me and suddenly dropped to his knees. Through howling tears he informed me his dad was moving away. This was news to me too and I was so upset for Tom. I was pulled between consoling him and ringing his father. I had played the role of both parents for years now and I was facing the prospect of having sole responsibility again. I contacted his dad who initially denied it and suggested it was just family rumours. But the rumours continued and we made plans to meet properly to discuss it. The three of us sat around a table at a local restaurant and after an hour of small talk, I asked the question: "Are you going away?"

"Yes," was his abrupt reply, "in two weeks, the tickets are bought." Tom went to pieces at the table and I held onto him to keep him upright. Tom was losing his dad and he made no effort to console him. I just held my son. Arrangements were made for him to see Tom that afternoon to spend some "quality time" with him before he was to leave in a couple of weeks' time as he would be busy packing. The decision was made; it was done and dusted with no further discussion. Tom would be left here fatherless.

No sooner had we started to come to terms with all this, we were hit with another emotional blow six months later. After 55 years of marriage, my parents decided to separate. My mum was to move down to the south west to live near my sister Sarah, and my dad decided to remain in the town. This was a great emotional upheaval. His health over time gradually deteriorated and I had taken on the responsibility of being his carer along with my full time work and raising Tom. I restricted my role to cleaning his flat, taking him shopping, plus taking him for hospital and doctor appointments. He was diagnosed with COPD (Chronic Obstructive Pulmonary Disease) resulting from a lifetime of smoking so the prognosis was bleak. This is a reason in itself that makes me glad I gave up smoking years ago and should serve as a big warning to others.

After my move back from Nottingham, I can't say any of my relationships had been very positive and had never evolved into me having the chance of becoming a wife or mother again. One true positive in all this though is my relationship with Tom, which has remained strong and we are very close. I was football "mum" for many years, trailing around the county with a muddy boy and muddy boots in tow. I can't deny that at times it has been truly difficult and we have struggled, but we managed to overcome all that life throws at you and I am proud to say that he never went without. When things were at their bleakest, there was an occasion when I went without food in order to buy nappies for him. I am very proud and did not want to burden other members of my family but when this was discovered they stepped in to help out. I had always dreamed of the large, happy family Christmas around the tree and dad carving turkey, but this was never meant to be. By raising Tom to be a good responsible adult, perhaps he can live the dream.

I am immensely proud of Tom who is in his second year at university, a place his mother did not get to! I started my own business over ten years ago, which has gone from strength to strength. I work very hard freelance bookkeeping and enjoy it very much, working both at home and work-based. The long-term clients I have worked for have now become very good and dear friends, as the relationship of work colleagues developed from their unending support of me throughout my cancer treatment.

I was already making plans for the end of the summer 2011, to streamline my work and spend more positive family time with Tom, when I had another blow in September 2011 which would take my life into a direction I had never thought possible. As I said, I didn't have any luck and a not-so-normal life. So let me tell you all about my journey and my run in with Peter Andre!

CHAPTER 2 – I'VE FOUND A LUMP

It was May 2011 when I felt a swelling in my left armpit and it was very tender to touch. I had started Zumba a few months before so I just presumed I had overdone it and maybe pulled something. I was only going once a week but was doing a week's worth of fitness in that single hour! So, I ignored it and got on with things, deciding that if it was still there in the next few days, I would go to the doctors. Then suddenly it disappeared as quickly as it had appeared. Nothing! All gone! Just like I had said to myself, I had overdone my moves. What am I like?

By June 2011, Darren and I returned from a holiday in Ibiza to the routine of work and Zumba classes. It was a popular class, so you had to keep to your own zone. On this particular occasion, I had two friends either side of me, and during one of our moves, we all took the wrong direction and I was hit from both sides. We laughed off the impact, and as I was re-adjusting my bra, which had dislodged in the incident, the instructor mouthed, "Are you OK?" I nodded my reply and continued with the class, although my upper arms, which had taken the brunt of the collision, were a bit sore, but I was fine.

On returning home I had a shower, and I decided, for no particular reason, to check my breasts. It was then I found a lump which I was pretty sure wasn't there that morning. I had watched a documentary a few years ago on how to check your breasts correctly. This always stayed in my mind and, now and again, I would check. To be honest, I didn't do it enough, and I'm guessing that the majority of readers of this are also guilty. Male and female!

It's terribly simple, not time consuming, and not enough people talk about checking breasts. Basically, when you are in the bath or shower, use the palm of your hands and fingers to rub around the breast. It's easier if you use shower gel or soap as they assist your hands in gliding around and you can get to know how everything feels so it's easier to spot any abnormalities. Checking your armpits is a good idea too, and should become part of your routine. I cannot advise on checking the male genitalia as I don't have any of my own, but it's not that hard to find the information these days!

I wasn't too shocked when I found a lump above my left breast. I immediately assumed that the incident at Zumba had caused an abscess, a cyst, or maybe it was just internal bruising from the impact as it was possible that the underwire of the bra had pressed into me. On this occasion I had not been wearing a sports bra. The lump didn't hurt but it was so pronounced that I could almost hold it in my fingers. Despite all this, I convinced myself that in a few days it would be gone. So, life continued as normal. Well, as normally as it did for me!

Although I had convinced myself it was nothing, I would find myself lying in bed pointing my left arm to the ceiling which seemed to expose the lump more. I was still convincing myself it was a cyst and that it wouldn't disappear overnight. Thoughts of cancer were immediately put to one side as I didn't feel ill. All this fuss over nothing!

By mid-August 2011, my eldest sister Tracey and I had booked a weekend treat at a spa. It was the first time for me so I was very excited. As it was a girlie weekend I thought that maybe this was my opportunity to discuss my thoughts with her to get a second opinion. I still wasn't really concerned, as with wearing my bra the lump was perfectly placed for the underwire, so in my mind I thought this was absolutely the cause. We were at the spa, bodies prepared within an inch of their life in order to put swimming costumes on, chatting to other ladies in the changing rooms so not a good time to bring the matter up.

We had thoroughly enjoyed the day and were feeling totally relaxed, when I headed off for my deep tissue massage. I hadn't had one before and found it painful. I hobbled back into the spa lounge and discovered with glee that I could almost turn my head all the way around like an owl, surveying all around me! But, gosh, it was painful and the left side of my back hurt for some time afterwards. We went for another swim, and all the time I was wondering when it would be an appropriate time to mention my 'lump' concern. Tracey went for her booked manicure and I thought that maybe when we were getting ready for dinner that evening I could mention it. Her manicure ran over slightly and we only just had enough time to get ready for dinner, so another opportunity missed. We started with champagne, had a lovely meal, and after a day of doing very little, realised we were exhausted and went to bed, sleeping soundly.

The next morning, my dad rang to say he was not well, so we cut the morning short so I could return home to see him. In the back of my mind I justified my decision to not bring the 'lump' conversation up with Tracey, as there hadn't been time and it could wait. I was still, sort of sure it was nothing and I didn't want to put a dampener on the weekend.

It was now August Bank Holiday weekend. Darren and I had been chatting, when I suddenly announced that I was worried about this lump I had discovered. We were in the bedroom and he asked to see it, so I took off my top and pointed to it. He barely even touched it but his face changed and he pulled his hand back. He was speechless for a second, then said, "You need to get that looked at." Now I was thinking, "If Doctor Darren thinks it's serious, maybe I should too." I still tried to talk down the seriousness of it by explaining the position of the underwired bra but he wasn't buying it. I already had an appointment at the doctors the following week for a repeat cervical smear test, so said I would mention it to the nurse. However, Darren was having none of it and demanded I make an appointment to see a doctor as soon as possible. Perhaps there was an element of not wanting it to be true, but I tried to reassure him that if the nurse thought it was serious enough she would call a doctor in. He was insistent though and demanded I arranged for a doctor to examine me.

On the Tuesday after the Bank Holiday, Tom was starting his first week of Sixth Form and after I dropped him off at school I rang the doctor's surgery. It still wasn't a case that I had accepted what the lump might be, it was more that Darren would only pester me later why I hadn't made the appointment. I managed to get an appointment the following day which was 31st August 2011.

A concerned Darren came with me but for me it was just another routine visit after having 18 months of repeat cervical smear tests and further investigations that kept coming back as borderline, high, abnormal, borderline results for the cells of the cervix. This is where the nickname, Doctor Darren, came from, as he had spent 18 months continually reassuring me that everything would be OK. "Listen to Doctor Darren," he would say if I started to worry that the test results would be serious.

My name flashed up on the appointment board and in I went. I told Darren he didn't need to come in with me, still convincing myself that a course of antibiotics would sort it. I explained to the female doctor all the previous events that had brought about this cyst. She asked me to remove my top and I sat facing her on the examining couch. My arms were up and out as I lay back. She was thoroughly checking both sides. I was told to get dressed and as I walked from behind the curtain she told me that she was referring me to the Glenfield Breast Care Centre. She said that as she did not specialise in this area she wanted it inspected further. I would be seen within two weeks because apparently there is a two-week turnaround if cancer is suspected. I just sat dumbfounded and said, "OK," and she reassured me that they would be able to tell me what it was. It was at this point she put her hand on my knee and said, "If it is malignant you will be in the best place to be looked after."

Wow, that was not what I was expecting her to say. I thanked her and said I would be back on Monday anyway for my three monthly repeat cervical smear test. Yippee! Every woman's favourite check up but one worth having! I walked back to the waiting room and made eye contact with Darren. I nodded my head towards the door to indicate that we were leaving and as we got outside I said, "I don't believe it, I have to go to Glenfield again."

It's not that I was not taking any of this seriously. I was not feeling ill and the lump did not hurt. I was not going to start panicking again over something that may never happen. Not with my health history anyway. The reference to visiting Glenfield again was because a year before I had been referred to Glenfield Heart Unit as I was having heart palpitations. A previous doctor from another surgery thought I had a childhood congenital heart defect because my ECG readings were so high. Over a matter of weeks I was having ECGs and an echocardiogram. The results were perfect and it was put down to stress. Oh yes, the palpitations had worsened after being told that I had a congenital heart problem, so my stress levels had increased and I changed doctors! But I was clear and that was fine. I was given a course of beta-blockers, which I decided not to stay on, and have been fine since. Also at this point no lump had been detected by the scans.

My visits to Leicester hospitals were not a rarity. As I child I had suffered bladder problems until age ten, so I was constantly visiting not only the nearest loo, but specialists and doctors at Leicester Royal Infirmary. At age four I was having my face repaired after the dog attack and at age 26 I was back at the hospital giving birth to Tom.

So, now I had to wait a fortnight for my appointment at Glenfield Breast Care Centre. I had days and nights for all sorts of thoughts to run through my head. I had just started the preparation of putting myself forward as a foster mother and for the time being this was going to have to go on hold. One thing that did prey on my mind was that if I had been having abnormal cervical smear results for 18 months that were detecting pre-cancerous cells, and now there is this thing in my breast, could I be diagnosed with cancer? As soon as this thought occurred, it was immediately cancelled by my other thought that, "No, course not, I didn't feel ill, people with cancer look and feel ill." I was most certainly not losing any weight! My shrinking clothes and weakness for crisps confirmed that!

CHAPTER 3 – GETTING MY BITS CHECKED

Within two days of my doctor's appointment, I received a letter from Glenfield Breast Care Centre for 8th September 2011 at 3.15pm. Enclosed was a leaflet explaining procedures and I read it despite being sure that a lot of it would not be applicable to me. I was still sure that I would be in and out within minutes, apologising for wasting everyone's time. There was a health form to fill out, with the usual personal girlie questions, so I completed it and stuck it on the fridge door for the following week.

The day of the appointment came and it was going to be easier to take Tracey with me, as Darren would have to go to work. So, after a light lunch together, we headed to Glenfield. We sat chatting and looking at magazines in the waiting room until my name was called. It was now time to get my bits checked. The nurse asked me to remove my upper clothes and put on a hospital gown. She then gave me a shopping basket to put my clothes into and sent me back to the waiting room. As I walked towards Tracey with my bright yellow shopping basket she asked, "Did you remember to get the milk and bread?" at which we both laughed, and I replied, "Sorry, I only got a paper!"

We chatted some more before I was called again and taken into a room for a mammogram. The radiologist explained more procedures to me but the one thing I remember hearing was, "You won't leave here today without knowing something." What a relief that was, at least I would have some idea what the lump was and whether where or when they could drain it.

The radiologist then asked me to remove my gown (which was very poorly tied) and to step forward to the mammogram machine, which I can only describe as looking like a huge meat slicer. She gently, but at the same time, quite unceremoniously, cupped my left boob and slapped it onto the coldest metal plate. It reminded me of a butcher slapping a steak on some weighing scales, "Just over half a pound, love!"

She explained that the plates come together to squash your boob so internal tissue can be seen. I had previously seen these on the television and remembered my mum describing how uncomfortable they were. Another strange thought occurred to me that I was too young for this. Older ladies don't really discuss the mammogram procedure, either because it's too embarrassing or it's not necessary to know too much about it until you have "reached a certain age." Perhaps it's boob taboo, or taboob! Just one of the many things you don't discuss with your mother like the "menopause" as its private, awkward, and only to be talked about when you're a fully signed up member of the older ladies club.

I was quickly brought back from all this mental joking to myself when the machine started and squashed my boob. Jeepers! Is the polite version of what I was thinking. Then before I had got my head around this technique it was suddenly time for the next one. Same again, slap it on and away we went again. Smile for the camera! It did occur to me, quite loudly in my head that they were going to burst if the machine squeezed them much harder. As soon as the machine started to release, I could breathe out with relief that it was all over, but oh no! We were now going for sideways shots. My poor boobs were now being squashed in the other direction. Holding still and leaning over the machine, like a man with his tie caught in a shredder, was the longest ten seconds of my life...that's ten seconds each time incidentally whilst holding my breath. The radiologist then explained to me that if anything unusual was spotted on the images that the machine had captured, the next procedure would be an ultrasound. I then put my gown back on, fiddling nervously with all the ribbon ties and returned to the waiting room.

I was smiling as I walked back towards my sister and was sure that everyone could see my now two perfectly cubed, freezing cold, boobs. We had a giggle about the whole thing while I made attempts to squeeze them back into shape, like dough, or at least try and warm them up again. No sooner had my bum touched the seat than I was called back again. This time it was for a blood pressure check, which thankfully was normal, and quite frankly, I was glad something was! The nurse remarked that I was the best-behaved patient she had seen all day and that I could come again, to which I laughed, said thanks, but that I would prefer not to.

Back to the waiting room again and I watched as various ladies, all ages, all sizes, came back to their waiting friends and relatives to say, "I've had the all-clear!" This was great, I thought, as I smiled at them, this is obviously part of the procedure and it was all new to me. I was pleased for them, the relief was written all over their faces and it occurred to me how well they would sleep that night with the good news. One came out and high-fived her husband, announcing her results to all in the waiting room. I smiled at her as I was sure that I would be going home soon with good news except not high-fiving her husband!

It's a strange waiting room. There is a sort of knowing, understanding feeling amongst all the people there and you feel a strong female bond even though you have never seen any of these ladies before. We were all strangers, but suddenly there was a collective support system and you immediately understood what this woman had been through to be there. For an Assessment/Investigation department it was and is a surprisingly busy waiting room too with lots of people, medical staff, friends, relatives, and ladies walking around in unflattering gowns and plastic shopping baskets. As I looked around I secretly hoped that most of them were check-up overspill from the mammograms on the other side of the reception, but now I know better, now I know they weren't.

"Clare Collins?"

I snapped back into reality as I was called again. Tracey kept standing up too and gathering her things as she wasn't sure if she was to come with me. The nurse indicated "no," and explained that I was off for an ultrasound. Maybe I should have been shocked, but I wasn't, you could see the lump quite clearly so it was not hard to figure out that there was definitely something there and I would need to be called back in.

CHAPTER 3 – GETTING MY BITS CHECKED

"See you in a mo," I said, as I left Tracey to read her out-of-date, dog-eared magazine, leaving my shopping basket with my best, but not sexy, going-to-the-doctor's bra, which had taken me an age to choose that morning, buried beneath my clothes!

I entered the small dimly-lit room and in the gloom, even before I had a chance to get in the door, the sonographer, who was to take the ultrasound immediately started talking to me, in broken English. I realised a nurse was present and looked to her for some help as I couldn't understand or hear what was being said and it was all going a little too fast. The door was still slowly closing, creaking as it did so and making the room even darker, so I wasn't catching anything that was being said. My eyes scanned the room and I saw my boob X-rays on the screen. Let's just say, this was the first time I had seen them like this. It's usually looking down on them being rather pleased with what you see, or maybe a little disappointed, or looking at them full-on the mirror, where you spend the next ten minutes lifting them up to where you think they should be! But here they were, in all their glory on a back-lit screen and my goodness, they looked fantastic! Perfect in fact, though I say it myself! Why didn't they look like that when I looked in the mirror? They were positioned exactly where they should be, or at least once were. A thought flashed through my mind that maybe I could ask to keep the pictures, show all my friends! My pride was suddenly brought up short when I realised what it was that was being discussed. On a second, closer look I realised that one of them had a dark patch on it.

The nurse, who at this point was also acting as interpreter, asked me to remove my three-ribbon gown. I felt strangely uncomfortable, standing in a dimly-lit room, with two women, being topless but with your jeans and boots still on. I clambered in an ungainly fashion onto the narrow bed, naturally tearing the thin, protective tissue, apologising as I did so. I lay back and had to raise my left arm, and within seconds the sonographer was applying the cold, greasy gel, which slips everywhere. The scanner was being pressed into, and around my boob and armpit so hard that I could hear the bed beneath me creaking, and pictured it, and me, crashing to the ground.

I had to twist, uncomfortably to my right and could see the ultrasound screen glowing to my side. The nurse tried to distract my "rabbit caught in the headlights" look by making idle chatter. The sonographer controlled the screen with a foot pedal which she was tapping continually. Then she moved to my right side and we were off again, but she was not concentrating as long on this side as she had on the left. She kept slapping more gel on and it was everywhere, even seeping its way into my long, dark wavy hair.

As always, ridiculous thoughts pop into your head, and I was silently cursing her for getting the gel everywhere because I would now have to go home and wash it all out even though we had made plans to go shopping on the way home. Well, that was all down the pan as she had made me all greasy. She was now back on my left side and she was going back over the same areas, the lump, my boob, my armpit. I could see the screen quite clearly now and it appeared both of us were mesmerised. Without eye contact, she said to the room, that they would need to do a biopsy.

"OK," I said, "when will I be coming back for that?"

"You won't be, you are going to have it now" she said in her broken English accent.

I glanced back at the screen and watched as she started to measure the dark, shaded area. The image switched back to my armpit and I could see other dark areas. The room was now silent and for the first time, without thinking, I used the words out loud,

"Do you think it is cancer?" to which I got no reply. Suddenly, the silence in the room was deafening. The atmosphere changed, it was palpable. Slowly, reality was hitting me in the face, my eyes moved upwards from the screen to a box sitting above it and hot, heavy tears started to roll from my eyes backwards into my hair and onto the ridiculously narrow bed with its torn protective covering. I didn't need an answer, I knew. This was it. I was staring cancer in the face. The deadly, silent killer that people talk about in hushed tones, was staring right back at me in all its dark ugliness. Despite the tears, my first thought was not one of self-pity or resignation, but instead, "You are not staying there, pal. One of us is going and it's not going to be me!"

So, this was it, this was me. I had cancer and to be honest I knew very little about it, except it was one scary word that no one liked. I was a 42 year old mother, daughter, sister, girlfriend, best friend, neighbour, director, work colleague, all the things that define me. The one, who despite everything that life has thrown at me, be it health or relationships, had always been OK. I always prided myself on being there for anyone who had a problem and offer counsel. Suddenly this was serious, proper grown-up stuff. Was I going to die? How am I going to tell my son, my family and all who mean so much to me? How am I going to leave this room in one piece? How long do I have left to live? Put all this apparent self-pity aside, the one thought that brought me the greatest sadness, was that of Tom standing next to my headstone with a simple "42 Years" carved onto it. It is the one thought that stayed with me over the next few months and beyond, that breaks my heart and still reduces me to tears today.

Self-pity over, grab back that fighting spirit. This is not right! They have it wrong! I know my own body. I rarely even come down with a cold. I grant you, there have been one or two scares along the way, but I dealt with it, sorted it and moved on. My body is a fighter, not a victim. This is what the smear tests kept detecting and if I do have cancer, am I going to die? I've just had my birthday and hardly celebrated it, so don't you think I would have pulled out all the stops and gone out with a blast? What about Christmas? Will I even see another Christmas? I had never been able to give Tom the big happy family Christmas with a table groaning with food, the type you dream of or see in the adverts, as life had been rather unfair to us and we were only now just getting on our feet. I had so much planned, so many thoughts of the future and now this. But I hadn't planned for this. No more plans to be made as I am going to die now. Not now please, let me live a bit longer so I can do more. But for all these questions I was not going to get an answer that day and although my mind was racing, I still hadn't had anything confirmed. As far as I was concerned, I was diagnosed and dead in the space of five minutes.

I had walked into that room a smiling woman and I would be leaving it a dying one

.

CHAPTER 4 – THIS WAS NOT IN MY LIFE PLAN

"The biopsy must go ahead immediately," I was told, as the procedure was explained to me. The plan was to take a sample of tissue from my armpit via a needle and a sample from the breast. For the first time since my big question, I started to frame sentences together again, rather than give one word answers. I had to explain that I was not good with needles, so when the sonographer asked if I wanted to see the needle, I gave quite a firm "No." Just to give you an idea of how this conversation was staged, I was still lying on my back with my left arm raised and bent behind the back of my neck, so my right hand could hold onto my left and hold my arm in place. I was told to totally relax, which wasn't easy with a sense of panic, to not talk, or in fact, to not move at all. If you're not good with needles either, you may want to skip down a paragraph, but as you're reading this anyway, I'm guessing you're not that squeamish.

My armpit was injected with anaesthetic and a tissue sample was taken. Then they anaesthetised the left side of my left breast. Each time the needle was used for the biopsy it sounded like a cap gun going off. It made a strange snapping sound as it quickly sucked out a piece of tissue. This happened three or four times and although it was only a few minutes it felt like forever. Suddenly, it was all done. The sonographer then proudly showed me the tissue samples in a small bottle by shaking it over my head. Hmm, not feeling great now! I thought it would be flakes of skin but they actually looked like bean sprouts. Sorry if you are eating your tea! Especially if you are eating bean sprouts! Once it was over, it was back into the complicated gown, which was even more difficult now as I was a little shaky, dry-mouthed, wet-haired and numb from the anaesthetic, so the nurse helped me to my feet, helped me with the gown and I returned to the waiting room.

As I walked out, the faces that had been smiling and full of hope before suddenly seemed so different. I gingerly walked back to my seat in pure silence, as the jarring of my footsteps sent a searing pain up the left side of my body. I was almost tiptoeing on a slant. My pale face was obviously speaking volumes, the pain, and the shock was there for all to see and all in the waiting room were avoiding eye contact. As I headed towards Tracey, she looked up and saw me – her face changed too. I sat down and suddenly I was chilled to the bone, absolutely frozen and shaking from top to toe. I was going into shock and calmly tried to tell her what had been going on as she tried valiantly to reassure me that everything would be alright. I think we both knew that from that moment on everything wasn't alright and about to change.

We sat for about ten minutes when another nurse called my name and this time came towards us. She suggested that Tracey came with me as it was time to see the oncologist. We followed the nurse into an examining room as she disappeared into an adjoining side room and reappeared with both the oncologist and some large dressings. He introduced himself and asked to examine me on the couch. I hesitated as I explained I had just had the biopsy and didn't really want him to touch me, let alone be there. As I had not had time to take any painkillers I was terribly uncomfortable but the nurse explained that she would take off my dressings, allow him to see what had been done, and then she would redress my wounds with new pads. I think I was more scared of him confirming it all again. I just wanted to say thank you very much for your time but I really don't want all of this. I have had a lovely day but I will just take the money thank you, and leave.

Sadly that scenario was not to happen as he pulled the curtains around the couch and once more, I climbed awkwardly, and with some difficulty now, onto the bed with my right arm and was aware that no-one was talking, or indeed making any sound at all. He took a keen interest in the area around the lump and asked if I had noticed anything different about my skin.

"Ah yes," I said, "my eczema has broken out."

"No," he said, "you have dimpling."

This is caused by the tumour clinging onto the breast tissue from within and drawing in the area around it, which causes a puckering look to the skin. Often referred to as orange peel. There was no doubt that my skin was being pulled in but it was almost around the side and towards my armpit so I could hardly see it.

This lump was hanging on for dear life and so was I!

The nurse re-dressed my wounds and asked me to get dressed. Both she and the oncologist went back into the side room and closed the door. Tracey was on the other side of the curtains and passed my clothes to me but had to help me dress as I could hardly move my left side without wincing. We sat alone and waited for what seemed like hours. We were chatting and even managed a nervous giggle, when we suddenly dropped silent. I looked at her and said, "This isn't going to be good is it?" Immediately, she tactfully replied, "Let's wait and see what they have to say."

The door opened and the oncologist and the breast care nurse came back in. They both sat on the examining couch leaning down towards me as we were on lower chairs. Neither of them said anything but instead were looking at me intently. It was as though they had asked a question and were waiting for my answer. I looked at them, confused, thinking "Did I miss something?" so I took a breath and asked the question, "What is it you are thinking?"

The oncologist clearly explained his findings, the lump, its texture, the positioning and the dimpling, "We suspect it is cancer."

An extended arm came across from Tracey to hold my hand but I couldn't move. It was like I had not heard what he had said and it was most certainly not going in! It was like life had just stopped. I felt like I was in slow motion and completely out of body. I asked every question I could think of, about it being a cyst, could it have been caused by the bra underwire, and repeating that I didn't feel ill. I was verbally trying to convince them, and myself, that this wasn't right, but it wasn't working. It was only a cyst for heaven's sake, how far-fetched can this be? They were wrong, I'm 42, I cannot have cancer. I was stemming the shock. He briefly explained the next steps that were to be taken and that it would still take another week to get the confirmation of the blood tests and the biopsy.

Well, that's it, this is for real. Suddenly, the tears came again, hot and heavy. Why couldn't everyone be in the room with me so I never have to repeat this to my family? How do you repeat this to your family? Tracey was talking to the oncologist and the nurse, but I couldn't hear them. I suddenly had tunnel vision. I was already shutting down. I had hit the brick wall and died right there. Actually it would be easier if I died right then and now. It would be less painful for everyone wouldn't it? Actually no, I didn't think that when I had a cold, why am I thinking it now? Everything seemed blocked out and my life was already over. Everyone was talking but it was muffled, like I was fainting. I looked at them and interrupted by asking, "How am I going to tell Tom?" I was in tears. Tracey explained to the nurse and oncologist that I was a single parent and Tom was my son. How unfair was this for him. I was becoming more and more upset. The oncologist turned to me and said that I was to stay in the room as long as I needed to and that if I had any more questions he was just next door.

I thanked him, and he left us with the nurse, who handed me some tissues from a box on the side and apologised in advance for them being really crap. Tracey was still talking to the nurse but I was not mentally in the room. I was just floating and staring at the socket on the wall. This wasn't real. This wasn't happening. This was like a film. It couldn't be real. Had I heard this correctly? What on earth was going on? I was supposed to be given antibiotics, talk about draining a cyst then go shopping!

Everything was changing, of which I had no control, and my

life had just stopped dead. I would occasionally snap back to what they were talking about and would just interrupt with another question. I found myself asking out loud how long I had left to live and what were my chances of survival. Panic was setting in. Everyone seemed calm except for me. Do something now, why are you talking? God help me. At this, the nurse jumped off the bed, leant into my face, put her hands on my knees, and said clearly and firmly, "We are going to get you past 80 years old. We are going to give you everything to make sure you survive. You have already started your treatment. You are in our care now and we are here for you." Those reassuring words made me break down again, but have stayed with me always. I can still hear her and see her staring into my face. These are people that didn't know me. They have no idea who I am, what I do, if I'm precious to anyone, yet they are taking my life into their hands and they are hoping to save it.

She was still discussing the procedures but all I could hear was the odd word, "surgery", "chemotherapy", "radiotherapy", "hair loss." All large, powerful angry words I'd heard before, knew what they were but didn't want any of them in my life. I felt like 'I' had just ended there and then. I suddenly had a reality check and I knew that this was the last chance I would have to ask all the questions that I would have in the following week as I waited for test results so I had to focus. My face was wet with a combination of tears and a runny nose, and as I had gone through nearly the whole box of tissues that I had been given, I started to search frantically in my handbag for a clean one. She kindly explained that I could telephone the centre anytime for anything, any questions, for any length of time. I imagine this is what happens when other women before me had had this news, go into a state of shock, and then realised they hadn't asked a million questions that they needed answers to. More so as you never expected that you would need to ask them. She passed me another box of tissues and we talked a bit more, but I can honestly say I have no memory of what about. I only remember asking, "When do I get the all-clear?" Sadly, no answer to that one.

It was now after 5.30pm and I had had enough, I wanted to leave, I had been prodded, poked and squashed. I was sore, exhausted and emotionally drained and just wanted to go home to my boy. I picked up my bag and coat and went to put the tissues back on the shelf but the nurse told me I could keep them. "No thanks," I said, "they are crap" and we all laughed. As I got to the door she stopped me and hugged me. It was such a simple gesture, but such a warm, caring gesture and it's a hug I will never forget. A hug at that moment I needed from a stranger who was going to help me survive and was reassuring me that I would.

She gave me a prepared box of cancer care leaflets with contact numbers and a card which had her direct dial telephone number. There would be no messing with the switchboard now, no being put on hold, or pressing the right number on the keypad, oh no, this was straight through direct contact. I was given an appointment card to attend the following week, 15th September 2011.

Tracey and I walked slowly out of the room and calmly down the corridor towards the main reception. The chairs were now empty, except for one lady in a wheelchair waiting for her lift. It felt like I was the one that day to be picked, everyone else got to go home. I wasn't high-fiving anyone.

As we got close to the main door the nurse came from behind me, suddenly calling my name and I looked round. My initial reaction was of complete relief. Oh my goodness, she is going to tell me that they have got it all wrong! As she caught up with me she hurriedly told me that I was to go for a blood test in the main building, but we had to hurry because they were due to close and it would give them all the information they needed to work on for the next week. OK, the last glimmer of a reprieve gone, and the start of endless forms and blood tests to come. Little did I know!

We walked into the main building and found the blood test area and the nurse wasn't wrong. The shutters were going down and record trolleys were being wheeled past us. We took a number and dutifully sat down to wait our turn as there were three people before us. We sat and chatted about nothing in particular and then I looked down at the form I was holding – "Test for: Cancer Present." I showed it to Tracey and said, "If this comes back positive, I'm disappearing. I'm not hanging around for all of this, I will just go away." She replied "You can't, they will want to treat you straight away." Crikey, she was not going to suggest some tranquil hideaway retreat and I was not going to get away from it. Even if I tried my lump was coming with me!

It was now 6pm and I was called in for my blood test. I was the last one of the day and the phlebotomist had some half eaten fruit pastilles on the side, "My husband will think I've got lost," she said.

"I am sorry, I am the last one," I replied. She looked on my form and could see I had come from the breast care centre. Whether this softened her, I don't know, but she kindly said, "Its fine, just a usual day." I looked at the fruit pastilles as I didn't want to look at the needle and said, "It looks like you've had your tea anyway," as I indicated with my eyes to the half-eaten packet. She laughed and I thanked her for taking the blood. As I walked out I hoped that cancer *wasn't* present in that test tube.

As we walked back to the car I know we talked, but again I have no idea what about, as I just remember being near the car when I realised the time. We hadn't checked the parking meter ticket as we didn't expect to be so long. But for the first, and only bit of good luck that day, we had no ticket and no wheel-clamp. My left side was really sore now and I still hadn't had any pain relief, so I took my bottle of water and painkillers out of my bag and sat on the passenger seat with the car door open. I saw my phone and sent a text to Tom to let him know we were on our way home. That was the first time I had never called him and heard his voice for fear of breaking down and him being too far away. I didn't want him to be far away, I wanted to hold him forever and never let him go. This was so unfair. I had to be here for my boy.

Tracey took the opportunity to call her husband and I heard her say, "They suspect its cancer." I knew then it was real, hearing it out loud again and I needed to call Darren. Although his shift at work would have just started, I dialled his mobile number praying that he would be able to take the call. It rang and rang, but no answer. Please God, let him be there. I dialled again and this time he answered. I was still not entirely with it and really don't remember the conversation except that I broke down when I told him what they thought they had found. I kept hearing his consoling words, "Bear, it's going to be OK." Bear was a nickname for me which was shortened from "Clare Bear" from childhood. His strength was just what I needed, it was almost like he already knew and had prepared himself. He told me he loved me and that I was to get home safely and that we would talk later on.

The message came that my brother-in-law sent his love, and we headed home. This was so unfair on all of us. Darren had lost his mother to cancer in 1989 – 21 days before his 21st birthday. It was going to open such old wounds for him and his family too and I was grief stricken. The people I did not want to hurt that I loved were the ones to be broken.

———

All I can remember discussing on the way home was how Tom was to be told. Tracey bravely volunteered to break the news but I knew that it had to come from me, and that I would be OK to tell him without losing it. We got home just before 7pm and decided to eat. We talked to Tom in the kitchen about his day and then he started to ask questions as to what had happened with me. I had no idea where my strength had come from to keep it together, but this was it, the one person I was truly dreading to tell, so I asked him to sit with me on the settee as Tracey stayed quietly in the kitchen.

I tried to keep my tone light, rather than laden with doom and gloom, and explained in practical terms what they had done, what tests they had carried out and what they suspected it was. I was determined not to break down and sob for fear of breaking his heart. But from somewhere my inner strength kept my tone level, positive and calm. I imagine this is the protective maternal instinct working at its best. He asked a few questions and I replied as best I could with the knowledge I had. It is paramount that you want to protect your child from being upset as a result of telling them something unbearable, all those subject areas you want to avoid like, someone has died, or your mother may have cancer. He seemed to take it all in his stride, hopefully feeding off my positive attitude and thinking that I looked OK, I sounded OK so surely I would be OK. This attitude was to be sorely tested in the coming months and in some ways what kept me sane.

Starvation kicked in and we ate like we hadn't eaten for days. We were exhausted and Tracey was ready to head home despite me being concerned that she needed to drive safely with all this buzzing in her head. I consoled myself with the fact that if she wanted to get upset, she could finally release her emotions in the privacy of her own home. She had been my backbone that day

---

and one of the reasons I had kept it together. Well, sort of kept it together!

Tom and I were now alone in the kitchen as I was clearing the plates. He stood in the doorway and, after spending the evening with his aunt and holding it all in, he was now able to pour out what he truly felt. He started talking rapidly saying how even though he was 16 he actually hadn't lost a member of his family. He had friends at school that had lost grandparents and some even a parent, but he hadn't lost a close relative so basically he wasn't ready for it. What would happen to him if he lost me? He vaguely remembered losing a great aunt when he was young, but had no conception of what was going on. He just remembered being distressed seeing other family members upset.

I stood right in front of him and had to talk over him continually reassuring him that I was going nowhere. I found myself saying things out loud to him that I had thought earlier in the day, I was too young and I was not ready to die. I AM NOT going anywhere. This thing was treatable and all of me was going to fight it. I had to be strong. I needed him to be strong. He had made me a mother and I was not planning on leaving him.

It seemed to work and it was all he needed to hear right at that moment. Everything your parents say in a child's eye is right. But then my secret concern was, had I promised the impossible? Had I promised him something which I couldn't achieve or deliver? I still had another week to wait for results and I had so much to sort out in the meantime. I hadn't even told the rest of the family yet.

But I knew, in my heart of hearts, that whatever was going to happen, I was going to have a damned good go at fighting this and I was determined to win. This was not in my life plan.

CHAPTER 5 – HANGING BY A THREAD

Breast cancer is something you hear about on television or read in magazines and you momentarily absorb the statistics. You may drop the odd pound coin in the collection box or buy something from the supermarket to support the campaign and presume the money reaches them and goes somewhere to do something. You think to yourself, "I'm not going to get it so why do I need to be more interested in it?" You may even have a friend or neighbour who takes part in the Race For Life, but still think that you're not old enough and none of your friends are old enough to get breast cancer, but you do your bit for charity. So, with all of this, why should you even give it a second thought or read up on it when, after all, you do the odd check in the shower if you remember?

I was no different, so I cannot begin to tell you the thoughts that flew through my head the day after the biopsy, except that I tried to make home life as normal as possible. I had slept pretty well, under the circumstances, but woke like I had something on my mind! Instantly remembering the day before. I think I spent most of the day trying to work out when and how I was going to tell the rest of the family. It was an experience I had not had to deal with before and I was at a loss and still in some state of shock. If you find out that you're pregnant you are bursting to tell everyone, knowing the happiness you will be spreading and eager to see the look on their faces. Delivering this sort of news is something completely different. I am the youngest of the family and I was going to break their hearts, it would change all of our lives for ever.

I decided, rightly or wrongly, to let my own head get around this huge blow and let Friday pass by. The longer I waited to tell them, the less I would be in shock, the more I could tell them in a calm and controlled way. It was possible that it would also be less time for them to have to sit on the news awaiting the final decision from the hospital tests. My decision to wait was also a selfless act – who wanted to hear bad news at any time, let alone a Friday night?

So, Saturday morning came and again I tried to keep myself busy. By 10am the postman had brought an official looking brown envelope and I knew straight away that it was from the hospital about my latest cervical smear test. Just how bad could this week get? The sight of these envelopes would become a regular occurrence over the next few months, but of course, at this stage I didn't know that. My eyes leapt around the letter in my eagerness to see what the results were and after 18 months of repeat tests the words in bold print that I had been waiting for – Normal. I couldn't believe it. It was all in the timing, and was it possible then that the cancer had not spread? I ran upstairs to tell Tom who didn't understand what I was jabbering away at as I waved a sheet of paper in his face. I knew Darren would be fast asleep at home as he'd finished his shift at 6am that morning and naturally, I couldn't tell the family just yet, so there was only one thing for it – the cure for all ills – go shopping!

As I got ready I felt all giddy and excited, almost as if I'd won the lottery and like all of this worry had gone away. I had filed away the fear and dread of what had occurred on Thursday for another day because that day it was all about me and I was going to get myself a faux fur coat. I'd seen it previously, tried it, liked it, put it back. But today, it had my name written all over it. It was only September, but what girl did not deserve a fur coat, even if it was a fake? I decided to splash out and buy myself some pretty underwear and some luxury shower gel too. Boy, did I know how to spoil myself? And why not? As I got to the checkout, the assistant looked in the basket, then at me and raised her eyebrows. I explained that no, reluctantly, it wasn't going to be one those weekends, it was just essential that I bought lacy underwear, posh smellies and a fur coat!

When I got home I was still on a high, and for those who know me, the way to celebrate that was to clean my house from top to bottom! I did some laundry and behaved as normally as I could, almost whistling as I worked. I'm a good whistler! I made arrangements to go and see my dad at 4pm and as I sat in the car outside his flat, reality brought me back from my high as I realised that I was about to be delivering some bad news and breaking another heart.

As a child, I had grown up hearing that friends and relatives of my parents were ill in hospital, or worse, had died. In many ways, having such a large family meant that you were well versed in receiving this kind of inevitable news. Now suddenly, I was the grown up, having to be the bearer of this news. My dad made some tea and as he put the cups down my panic set in. There was no turning back, no making up some other pretence for being there, I had to go through with it. I felt a bit light-headed as I knew I was going to have to deliver the bad news quickly and clearly. I was OK and I was going to get through this and hope that the positive news quickly outweighed the bad.

I rattled out everything that had happened. As I watched his shocked face, I continued talking by including that I was young enough and strong enough to fight it. I reassured him that with every last breath in my body I would be fighting and I explained about the chemotherapy and the hair loss. I saw him casting his eyes over my hair, which at this stage was down to my waist, "It's hair Dad. It will grow back!" As much as I wanted to leave as the room felt like it was closing in on me, I knew that I couldn't leave him just yet and needed to give him a bit more time to let all this sink in and ask any necessary questions. We continued to chat and I kept my voice at a normal level so as not to cause any more concern than was necessary. I asked him not to contact my mum as I wanted to tell her myself and I would be doing that as soon as I got home. I wanted her to hear the news from me and was only sorry I couldn't do it face-to-face as she was living in the south west, and it would have to be done over the telephone.

An hour later, I was back at home and quickly ran over the conversation I would have with her in my head. She was pleased, and a little surprised to hear from me on a Saturday evening, and I was worried she would launch into lots of small talk which I would have to interrupt. I needed to get this out and it needed to be quick. I checked she was sitting down and could sense that she assumed it was bad news about my dad. I then went into autopilot and recited, pretty much word for word, the events that I had described to my dad. All I could hear was "No, No, No." Oh heck, this wasn't good, but I reassured her over and over that I was going to fight it and that I was going to be OK. She said that she never thought any of her daughters would ever get anything like this, particularly the youngest. So I decided to flower it up, if at all possible, as I had done with my dad, that there was good news, the cervical smear test was normal. I don't think either of them had heard this remark as the bad outweighed the good.

I was emotionally drained and couldn't face breaking the news to anyone else in the family just yet. I asked my mum to break the news to Sarah, as they lived within a mile of each other. She waited until the following morning. Sarah was watching the rugby on the television as she was told by telephone and just switched the TV off and sat looking at the screen. When her husband, Bruce, came in to find out why it had gone all quiet he asked what was wrong and she told him. He sat, staring at the same screen and just said, "Shit, that's serious." The reaction was the same from everyone, utter shock and disbelief. Clare Bear was going to need all the help, love and support she could get.

When I got home I had messaged three of my friends to see if they were available for coffee that evening. One was away for the weekend but sensed there was something wrong and called me straight back, "What's up bud?" When I realised she was so far away I knew I couldn't palm her off with a "Nothing, everything's OK," so instead I said, "I didn't want to tell you this by phone, but I may have breast cancer." She responded in her usual strong consoling way with words that have stayed with me, "We are all here for you bud. We all love you!" I didn't hear from the others straight away and assumed, as it was early on Saturday evening, they were busy. No matter, it could wait.

Not long afterwards, I got a call and texts from them. We arranged to meet properly on the Sunday for a good long talk, but I quickly outlined the facts to ease their apparent horror at my news. The calm strength I was experiencing was overwhelming as I reassured them and found myself concerned that they take time to do the necessary checks on their own breasts as this was a wake up call for all of us. I still had so many more people to tell, so it was going to be a long few days. Where was all this strength coming from?

I had spoken to one of my primary clients, but asked him not to say anything to anyone else just yet. My best friend worked with us and she thought I was taking a bit of time off to look after my dad, and that maybe I was just feeling a little bit under the weather. I wanted the news to come from me but as I had not yet had it officially confirmed I did not want her to worry unnecessarily. We agreed I would work from home. Again, I needed her to enjoy her weekend. Holding out for a few days would benefit her. It didn't matter to me, I already knew and she had her own dealings with her mother and her cancer treatments.

The following week was a strange time and I kept myself hidden. I avoided speaking to anyone, I avoided the neighbours and avoided going anywhere where I might bump into people I knew. I continued working but stayed at home, I set about spring cleaning and painted the conservatory. In many ways, I was preparing my nest and getting my life and my home in order. I needed that time for myself, time to gather my thoughts and protect myself from what lay ahead. Painting was mind-numbing so I was able to think. While it occupied me I was still deep in thought, and anyway, if I was given only months to live, at least the house could be packed up and sold, with no effort from anyone else. I was determined that no-one would have to have the worry and trouble of clearing the loft! Drawers and cupboards were cleared and organised so if family had to pack and sort everything, it would be where it should be. I had visions of my sisters on their knees pulling things out of cupboards, and holding them up asking "What did she keep this for?"

By Wednesday, I was mentally and physically drained, but prepared. It was 14th September 2011, and as I was getting ready for bed and receiving the official results the next day, I wanted to be as well rested as I could. I didn't want to be hanging by a thread any longer.

CHAPTER 6 – IT'S ALL GONE TITS UP!

My appointment to get the results wasn't until 4.15pm. Gosh, it was going to be a long day. Tracey and Darren were coming with me but I insisted that Tom should go to school as it was not an environment I wanted him to be in. Everyone was tense. It felt like we were preparing to go to a funeral, all making idle small talk, but dreading what was to come and secretly keeping an eye on the time. There is only so much tea one can drink. By now, I had all but convinced myself that I had cancer and had spent most of the week trying to convince those close to me of the same outcome so that it would lessen their shock. They had told me in the Breast Care Centre that they suspected it. "They suspect it" rang through my head. It has to be.

We arrived at Glenfield, entered the Breast Care Centre, and my nerves were on a knife's edge. Next time I'd be walking back through these doors, I would have the results. It's odd what your head does to you at times of extreme stress. Everything looked different. I was picking out ridiculous inane details, the pattern on the wallpaper, the edges of the floor tiles and the details on people's shoes. I decided to try and distract myself by flicking through a magazine. But I was far too anxious and experiencing a strange out-of-body experience. Time had once again slowed down and my palms were sweating, I was dry-mouthed and I was aware that my breathing was laboured. The nerves were taking over and I couldn't sit still, so would suddenly stand and walk around the room reading the notice boards and looking at the faded framed pictures of landscapes in a vain effort to take my mind off where I was. There weren't many people there at this time of day, only a few ladies in their hospital gowns. Poor loves. Poor me.

I had read every notice on every board and paced up and down the corridor. I suddenly took in something I had read before, but which hadn't registered – there was an hour's delay to the appointments. Jeez no, not today. An hour seemed like a lifetime. Patients were coming and going, names were being called, and staff were walking up and down and disappearing into side-rooms with patients' folders, so it wasn't like there wasn't anything happening. I went to speak to the receptionist, "Hi, I'm waiting for my results today. Do you think they will be long?" She looked up and said, "They have your paperwork, sorry, we are facing a bit of a delay." There was no point in starting a fuss, everyone was busy, I could see that, and frantically raising my voice wasn't going to speed anything up. I looked at her with polite resignation and went to sit down.

As my bottom reached the seat the panic surged up inside me and I just wanted to run down the corridor and back to the car. I just wanted someone to tell me yes or no. Simple really. I glanced down the corridor and saw the closed doors. In one of those rooms was my folder with my results. The rest of my life was on a piece of paper. If I had a life, of course. Surge of panic again.

Almost an hour later, at 5.10pm my name was called. I practically sprinted down to the room, tripping over my own feet, with Darren and Tracey trailing behind, trying to keep up. The nurse who had called my name, stopped in the doorway and turned to say, "Only one of you can go in with her." I turned to look at both of them. How on earth was I going to choose? I turned back to the nurse and said, "I am prepared to take them both in, or not go in at all." She looked at me and said, "OK," and we all walked in. The room was tiny and the head surgeon was at a desk. The breast care nurse sat behind her. We were facing them and behind us, by the door, stood another breast care nurse. Six of us all squeezed in, it was almost comical, and just as well no-one was claustrophobic! If they were, now was not the time to voice it!

The surgeon introduced herself in a very headmistress-like manner and we sat in silence. She knew who I was; she didn't need to know who my companions were. She asked me to clarify what I had been told the week before and in a nervy, shaky voice I explained that they suspected it was cancer. She was looking at me over the top of her glasses, glancing down a couple of times, as I spoke, at my notes which lay before her. When I had finished my brief explanation, she looked up and said:

"I can confirm it's cancer."

Just like that. No preamble, no theatrics. Just like that. Now, please remember, that I had been through the mill a bit lately and

---

in many ways thought I had prepared myself to hear this. But, I was wrong. So wrong. I was not prepared at all, and out of my mouth, quite involuntarily, came a weird cry. My eyes instantly filled with hot tears, and I searched for the tissues in my bag. I couldn't look at anyone. I didn't want to see their faces, I didn't want them to see mine. It wasn't fair that they had to hear this. It wasn't fair that anyone had to hear it!

I was still fumbling in my bag, desperately seeking out the tissues I had put in earlier. The surgeon turned to the nurses and demanded "Can someone get this lady some tissues please?" They jumped to her command, but by now I had found them. All I wanted to hear now was that the cancer had not spread. She looked back down to the notes and said, in quite a matter-of-a fact voice, that when they perform surgery they would take some lymph nodes to check whether or not the cancer had spread. So, I had no answer to that one yet. She flicked through some more notes and, without looking up at me, read my blood test results out loud:

"Your bloods are…clear."

This time, I let out a groan and then looked at my support group. Darren took my hand and Tracey nodded to me. I could finally breathe because even though I now knew I had cancer, life was still going to be OK. It was confirmed I had left breast carcinoma with associated DCIS. The most common form of breast cancer! But it was still unwanted, whatever form it was! Immediately, we started to discuss surgery and I had the choice between a lumpectomy (removal of the lump but medically known as a wide local excision), or a mastectomy from that day's menu. She explained that I was going to be taken to a quiet room to make my decision and I was handed two booklets on both procedures. Oddly, on our way out she said something that has always remained with me: "The only way you will get through this is with a sense of humour!" I replied with a smile, "Oh well, I will be OK then!" to which we all agreed. At that point in time, it felt like my humour was the only thing I had left. Cancer couldn't touch that.

We were taken next door to a reasonably pleasant room with low lighting and comfy sofas. The breast care nurse came with us and we all slumped down, breathed out and started discussing my surgery options. I had a strange sense of relief, even though the news was not good. Whichever way I went, chemotherapy was a certainty. On my brief swotting up on the subject beforehand, this was the one thing I was really hoping to avoid. Even the word seemed angry and intrusive and frightened me. The mastectomy was far too much for me to consider and the nurse explained that if this major surgery was necessary I would not have been offered a lumpectomy.

I voiced my concerns that if I went for a mastectomy on my left breast I didn't want to discover at a later date that it didn't need to be done. There was no going back on that one. The nurse then, out of the blue, but kindly suggested that I may want to get my hair cut shorter. I loved my hair. I was known for my thick dark hair and was gutted, but this was the just the very start of a very long journey. So, the cancer was creeping up and taking all of my femininity. Deep breath. Do you know what? Bring it on. This fight had already started and I was going to win, whatever cancer decided to throw at me. I was going to have to fight many battles in order to win this war and it had hurt many people around me already.

All three of us asked every question we could think of by the time the other nurse had come in and asked if we were ready to go back in. I was just hoping that my decision was the right one.

—

How was I to know? What if I had a lumpectomy and was then told I should have had the mastectomy? This was my decision, no-one could make it for me. They could only give me advice.

I went back in to see the head surgeon on my own. Tracey wanted to take a bit of time out in the corridor to absorb what had happened and Darren decided to wander back up to the waiting room. We'd gone from waiting over an hour, to being bombarded with information, and now we all needed a bit of time to sort it out in our own heads. The surgeon asked if I'd decided and I said, "Lumpectomy please," and felt like I should have added, "with a side salad and a large coke!" I even said please!

She started to look through her diary and suggested three weeks' time on a Friday. I replied I was free. I was hardly going to look in my diary and say, "Sorry, I've got something on that day, how is the week after looking?" Three weeks suddenly seemed an awfully long time and I asked whether leaving the cancer that long could cause it to spread further in the meantime. I can only think she misunderstood what I was saying and thought I'd asked whether the cancer would spread if I didn't have the surgery. She then launched into some medical-speak and lost me completely. Now I was wondering if I'd made the right decision.

A different surgeon would be performing the operation, because if it was a mastectomy, she would perform it. When she said his name, the breast care nurse who had resumed her seat behind her put both thumbs up. Yay!

So that was it! I was sorted. I was booked in and signed up to the new cancer club membership for my wide local excision and axillary surgery. I had signed the consent form for "Removal of Cancer." I would require a pre-assessment and this would be part of it to get me cancer-free. I still had to get through the next three weeks and just hope that the cancer didn't spread any further in that time.

I found out later that Darren had inadvertently overheard a conversation between the receptionist and a nurse at the front desk. The receptionist had asked a nurse how it was going, indicating the room I was going into. "Not good," the nurse had replied. I think it shocked him to the core and hearing it out loud again only confirmed the devastation. He had already known what we were heading for.

I had finished making arrangements with the surgeon and as I walked back into the corridor, I saw Tracey sitting there. She looked emotionally exhausted. I smiled at her, reassuringly, and as she looked at me I could read her thoughts – her baby sister had cancer and this was a long journey that I was about to embark on with no guarantee of success and in many ways I had to walk it alone. I could read her thoughts because this was what I was thinking too.

We then walked towards Darren who was sitting further away and he too looked drained. I was responsible for hurting all these people. Why couldn't it just hurt me? This was only the beginning in the waiting room and it had all gone tits up; it was the tip of the iceberg. I had so many other people to tell – where do you start? I was going to have to confirm it to my parents that their youngest child had cancer, to Sarah that her sister had cancer, and, talking of children – I was going to have to tell my son which was worst of all. How unfair was that?

CHAPTER 7 – SQUATTERS' RIGHTS!

I had three weeks to prepare myself, and my life, for cancer surgery. I had signed a "contract" with the hospital for removal of cancer from the left breast and I had made it quite clear that if they found that more needed to be removed then they had my permission to do so. I wanted to be free of it and if it meant that I had to lose more of my body to make this happen then I was prepared to do it. However, they wouldn't accept this and pointed out that they would have to sew me back up, wait until I had come round from the anaesthetic and then discuss further options. NHS guidelines stipulated that they were only allowed to action what I had signed on the consent form. They were taking it step by step, rule by rule, I just wanted this "squatter" out of my breast as it had no right to be there no matter what it took.

That was the stage I was at. I had begun to see the tumour as an interloper, the enemy, not necessarily giving it a name but certainly personalising it by giving it a character. A character I hated and wanted rid of. It didn't deserve a name or recognition. I was already starting to get used to living with it. Everywhere I went it had to come with me. I hadn't given it permission to move in, I hadn't been given the option, and now this squatter had rights. I had not planned or discussed the situation of us residing together, and I most certainly did not remember discussing the house rules. There were to be no happy times with this new arrangement and I had my work cut out to ensure it left by whatever means whilst it sat back and "clung on."

I had arrangements to make as I still needed to maintain the life I had prior to all this. I was in for a slow recovery so I wanted to make sure that all of my clients' work was up to date and that my home was in order. I am a freakishly organised person at the best of times, but this time I was on a mission: shopping, cleaning and laundry was to be done within an inch of its life. Other medical preparations had to be done too, with additional health check-ups and the removal of a contraceptive coil by my GP. That's a little bit personal, but as we're on the subject, with a rapid growing and aggressive tumour feeding off my body's oestrogen an "assisting contraceptive participator" was not an option, so he was the first one to be ejected from my body.

I am also a user of contact lenses, and although I was not planning on viewing the surgery, they would not be allowed anywhere near the operating room, so I had to update my glasses prescription. I had my appointment at the opticians, and had the usual jumping and squealing reaction to the puff of air to test your eye pressure. No matter how much you expect it, you are still taken by surprise. After I'd jumped, squealed and sniggered, the optician didn't even smile, so I can only presume I'm not as unique as I'd like to have thought and that the optician had numbed themselves to this reaction that happens 20 times a day.

I ordered my smart and trendy "don't I look clever" glasses and a week later had arranged a fitting. If you do not wear either glasses or lenses, with contact lenses you cannot wear your everyday glasses over them because you would have a double prescription and everything becomes a blur again. Special prescription glasses are obtainable though to wear over contact lenses. Just for the record! The young assistant sat opposite me, and as I had arrived wearing my contact lenses, I put on my new glasses just to see how they fit and with blurred vision I peered into the mirror. I could just make out one dark eyebrow, mine, protruding above one of the lenses. I pointed out that they weren't level and I said, "I must have wonky ears."

The assistant asked, "Do you want me to straighten them up?"

I asked, "What, my ears?"

Gosh, I'm hilarious, and thankfully she saw the humour in it too and laughed with me. She then altered my glasses, left my wonky ears where they were and took £60 from me for the privilege. No discount for the comedian then?

The next task was my pre-assessment at Glenfield Hospital, ten days and counting before the surgery. I was weighed (it is never what you want it to be) and height measured. I tried lying and said I was 8ft 4" to counteract the weight. Then my temperature and blood pressure were taken and I had a nice long questionnaire to complete. A nurse then thoroughly explained the procedure of the operation and went through an extensive list of what I could, and could not do, after the surgery.

I had given this some thought and read plenty of pamphlets to get a gist of the rules: no ironing, no vacuuming, no lifting wet laundry, or weights of any kind – anything that would put my upper torso under any pressure really. I told her that this would be difficult as this constituted the majority of my role as a home-maker, but she insisted that this role would need to be assigned to someone else and I could "reclaim" it after I had recovered. This was taking more of my feminine role as mother and home-maker away. I was having lymph nodes removed from my left armpit and was only now understanding what they do. The removal of them can lead to lymphoedema.

This means that the arm can swell with fluid, at any time, for the rest of my life. I cannot chew my fingernails, I must not let any steam from boiling water (i.e. a pan or kettle) touch my arm, I should wear insect repellent in the garden and cover my arm to prevent bites, and I should wear high factor sun cream (SPF 50-60). In the event of any cuts to the arm it should be treated immediately with antiseptic. I am never to have blood taken or blood pressure from this arm because of the blood pressure cuff. If I take any flights, I should wear a compression sleeve. The list went on, and on.

Then, like a bolt out of the blue, she unexpectedly asked how I felt "as a woman." This was the first time someone had asked me this question, and for the first time, after being bombarded with medical jargon and dos and don'ts, I felt someone was actually asking about me and my emotions. It was not difficult for the tears to surface again. All the thoughts that had been swimming in my head the last few weeks, which I had not shared with anyone, all my innermost emotions rather than practicalities, were just waiting to burst forth. I had done a lot of research by now, both into my diagnosis and my treatment, both now and in the future.

It had crossed my mind, too many times, that it was time for Darren to find himself a healthy, cancer-free woman so that he wouldn't get dragged down with me and be constantly reminded of the loss of his mother to the same disease. We did not know at this stage if I was actually going to survive.

Our relationship was never destined to end happily ever after as he had made it clear that he preferred to be on his own with no commitments. I had made it equally clear that I did not want to be alone and this was a barrier that we both reluctantly accepted, and in its own way, the relationship sort of jogged along for years. But this new layer to the ever-present barrier was not going to help the relationship run any smoother.

I was facing potential ugly scarring on an important area of my femininity and the question of who would want to be with a woman whose breasts bore disfiguring scars was haunting me. There were plenty of women out there with perfect health, perfect breasts, although not a lot think that, and I had fallen into that stereotypical place that this was important to a man and it was now something I would be unable to offer. Any thoughts of looking in the mirror and liking what I saw were long gone for the moment, and certainly any thoughts of feeling sexually attractive were non-existent. So my list of reasons for Darren to stick around was getting less and less by the day. At the same time I was very aware that he could meet a "perfectly healthy woman" who in time could also be diagnosed. A risk we all take in love. But above all of these reasons he was sticking around for full support, regardless of the consequences and simply had no interest in scars or leaving me because my breasts would not be intact.

All of these negative thoughts were not improved by my next meeting with another nurse who booked my bed, and showed me the "Redivac" drainage bottle that I would be fitted with after surgery. Eeeerughh! Can it get any worse? Yes, it can, particularly if you're eating right now, you may need to look away and skip to the next paragraph. After surgery, a tube is fitted and held in place by stitches, which drains away any excessive fluid from the breast that the body cannot get rid of itself. This is particularly important if some of the lymph nodes have been removed, as this is what they do, as part of the body's natural drainage system. The fluid then drains into the bottle, which is prettily hidden in a nicely stitched flowery bag which you carry on your shoulder. Not quite the accessory every woman wants, but a bag all the same. The drain is only fitted for a few days and then it's removed.

Outwardly, I appeared calm and collected. I was not running around the room screaming, but inwardly, the stress of all this was taking its toll. Just to add to my current "not feeling beautiful" state of mind, my eczema had broken out, most of it on my torso. I had been a mild eczema sufferer for years, where it rarely made an appearance and now it was making itself known with gusto. It had got so bad at one point, that after a bit more research, I convinced myself it was ringworm. Well, why not? I had everything else! There was some medical concern and it had to be checked as my eczema is a rare form and not your everyday one, as I could not have broken skin or open wounds prior to surgery as these would make me prone to infection. Thankfully, my body didn't let me down with this one, and it was on the road to recovery, which meant that it would be cleared up in time for surgery.

So, just when I thought I had ticked every box I was presented with one further procedure. For the surgeon to correctly identify the first few lymph nodes, I had to have a radiation injection. This is medically called sentinel node localisation. This meant yet another appointment in my now bulging diary, and was booked for the day before surgery at Glenfield Hospital. During the operation the surgeon would apply some dye which would detect the first few nodes by the radiation. He described them as being like tangled Christmas tree lights sitting in the armpit and for him to find the first few would be pretty much impossible. Therefore, the application of the blue dye hits the first few, making them more detectable.

So, Darren came with me to this appointment, and as we sat in the waiting room I was given yet another questionnaire. I was called in and Darren came into the room with me. I stripped to the waist and put on a gown. As I lay on the bed, which looked rather like a dentist chair, the nurse began to explain the procedure. She had gloves on and a box with a skull and cross bones printed on the side, not scary at all! She injected the radiation next to my left nipple with the usual stupid comment about it feeling like a small scratch. Are you kidding me? Aaarggh! Four letter expletives do not cover what was going through my mind right then. Extreme, intense pain was searing through every nerve in my body. There is a lot to be said for anaesthetic.

As Darren was constantly reassuring me through this ten second (seemed like ten years) procedure, I was squeezing his hand so hard that his fingers were going blue. His eyes were flicking from the procedure, back to my face, and he did everything he could not to wince. He too was clearly in pain and I think he felt every inch of what I was feeling. I wanted to bat the nurse way, tense everything up, anything to take the pain away. I couldn't look – there was a needle, and a big one at that! Finally, after the ten excruciatingly long seconds, the pain was over. She gave me a few minutes to recover myself in case I felt faint or nauseous then I got dressed. I felt surprisingly OK and we were allowed to leave.

CHAPTER 7 – SQUATTERS' RIGHTS!

Everything was now set for 7am the next day. My bag was packed, my alarm was set, my pre-surgery sterile wash was sitting by the shower and my house was spotless. I had signed the bailiff's papers to evict my squatter and his rights!

CHAPTER 8 – OPERATION CLARE

The day had arrived and I was up at 5am showering with my sterile wash which was to be used on my body and on my hair. No breakfast, because naturally I was fasting, but why is it when you're told not to eat, all you can think about is food? My bag was packed and I was ready to head off to the hospital. I was trying to keep busy to stave off the nerves jangling around inside me and to stop myself from thinking whether or not I was going to come out of this alive. Would I ever come home again?

We had arranged that the night before, Tom would stay at Tracey's house. Attending school would be pointless for him, as he wouldn't concentrate and then he would have to come home to an empty house. It had also occurred to me that he would have family around him when he got the news from "Operation Clare," and of course, more practically, if the worst did happen, he would be surrounded by family rather than sitting alone. This wasn't something that I really wanted to contemplate, but I had to be sensible.

At 7am, Darren and I arrived at Glenfield Hospital and followed the directions for the ward that the nurse had given to us. I was shown to my bed and I was surprised that the ward was so lively with the patients. At this time in the morning I thought everyone would still be fast asleep, but of course, if you've ever stayed in hospital you would know that everything starts at 6am, the tablet trolley, the blood pressure monitors and, of course, the ceremonial morning bathroom visit.

Darren sat in the high, uncomfortable chair next to the high, uncomfortable bed which I was now awkwardly sitting on. We played with the controls for a while until I was comfy, switched the light on and off and decided not to pay for the television just yet. I had a few visitors to keep me occupied, starting with the breast care nurse who took my temperature and blood pressure and asked me a series of questions about potential allergies. Ha, where do I start – sticking plasters, wasp stings, jellyfish stings (not a potential threat in surgery hopefully), oh, and the sterile wash which I had been forced to use. My skin took an instant dislike to it after being used the night before and that morning. My eczema was screaming at me and I needed my hands taped into oven gloves to stop myself from scratching my skin off.

They measured my ankles to assess which hospital stockings I needed to wear, pre-, during and post-surgery. Again, if you've been in hospital you know these are the least fetching things to wear and are also the tightest things in the world which are the very devil to put on. I cannot understand how these things are good for you. Each visitor to my bed asked the same question: name and inmate number. Oh no, hang on, that's name and date of birth. Same thing in many ways, I was beginning to feel like a prisoner anyway.

The lady in the bed next to me was sitting up and was fitted with a lovely drainage bottle. She had discreetly hidden it beneath her bed jacket and looked happy sitting there watching the world go by. The lady opposite was chatting to the nurse who was arranging her tablets into a little plastic cup. These two women had had their surgery the day before and here they were sitting up, chatting and laughing as if they'd had an ingrowing toenail removed instead of major breast surgery. Suddenly, this was a rather good advertisement for what was about to come and maybe I shouldn't be so frightened. That would be me tomorrow, well, let's hope that is me tomorrow. Minus the bed jacket!

The lady opposite was having her breakfast, which, despite being hospital food, looked and smelt fabulous – remember, I'm desperately hungry by now and would eat anything – including hospital food. Curtains were being pulled around the beds and she took the opportunity to come over to me and chat. She quite openly explained that the day before she had had a double mastectomy, just like that, as if was an everyday occurrence. Thankfully, I didn't need to think of anything to say because she then asked what I was in for – another reference to a prison!

I explained that I was here for a lumpectomy, which now seemed nothing compared to her operation. She perched on the end of the bed and told us that she would soon be 92 and not doing so bad for her age. She received raised eyebrows and congratulations from us then went back to her bed to pick up framed photographs of her family. She returned to my bed and went through who they all were. As she rattled through various children, grandchildren and great-grandchildren, one picture slipped out of the frame and onto my bed. I picked it up and secured it back in its frame while she told us how wonderful her daughters were. All I could think of as I put the picture back that here she was all upbeat and positive and she was looking at this pale faced nervous wreck, hoping that one day she too would be showing off pictures of her grandchildren. She then said, "All you need is courage," and I replied, "And a smile."

It was a moment of clarity. There I was, sitting with a woman more than twice my age, with this huge family, who had been through so much already and was being incredibly brave. It was people like her that would get me through. She gathered up her photographs and started to return to her bed, and then, as she turned to walk away, she did the most incredible thing. No, it wasn't passing on any more words of wisdom, instead, she passed wind, very loud and very long. I thought maybe she would turn round and apologise, or at least do a snigger with embarrassment, but no, nothing, no indication that she was even aware of what she had just done. I turned my head to look at Darren to see if he had heard it too, but I didn't need to ask, my answer was right there, his shoulders were shaking and his eyes streaming with tears desperately trying to hold in his laughter. But, her breaking wind perhaps did something else, she broke the ice on my fear, and suddenly I wasn't quite so frightened any more.

Once the air had cleared, literally, my next visitor was the surgeon's assistant. This was a very young female who wore a low cut top with two pert little breasts popping out over the top. That's right, the last things I needed to see! Trying not to look down I concentrated on her face as she went through some of the

—

procedure and then left, only to come back with the surgeon and what I assumed to be, a student doctor. The curtains were drawn and they said they wanted to examine me. The surgeon sat next to me on the bed and took my hand, instantly shaking me into the reality of the moment. He explained the procedure in a bit more detail and then started to draw on my breast with a marker pen where the cuts would be made. He asked me if I would consent to the student doctor examining me and I thought, well, they've got to learn, why not?

Despite the seriousness of what was going on, it still made me think of the almost ridiculous nature of the situation, everyone was politely silent and a complete stranger was handling my boob. It made me want to laugh out loud as I did everything I could think of to take myself out of the situation and not catch his eye. When the surgeon had finished "drawing" on me, he "signed off" by drawing a smiley face on my chest. It briefly lightened the moment but made me realise that this man was a total stranger. This was the first time I had met him, and I was placing all my faith in this man to take away the cancer. It's a strange relationship, complete strangers joined inextricably by such a high level of trust. I was to be the second patient to undergo surgery that morning and as they started to walk away, the surgeon gave me one last look and said that he would see me soon. He was so caring and I felt shaken. A panic came over me. A perfect stranger had just handled my breast. I demanded that Darren stick his hand up my top to be the last one to feel the breast as it was! Like it was flipping important! In a strange kind of panicked way, looking at this crazy woman sitting on the bed covered in marker pen…he did!

The next to arrive was the anaesthetist, someone you really had to trust that they knew what they were doing. He checked my inmate details and asked what sort of anaesthetic I would like. Wow, who knew you could choose? I asked him what my choices were and he said, "A regular injection, a mallet or a hammer." That's right, a hilarious anaesthetist, great. I opted for the injection as I wasn't sure I trusted the other two. This sense of joviality was taking the sting out of the seriousness of the situation and it was helping. Just a pity that I had to go through with the surgery and couldn't just sit there all day cracking jokes. Their empathy to my situation was reassuring, they were aware that having a major cancer operation is nerve wrecking so adding a bit of humour to lighten the mood was vital. This could potentially be the last laugh I was having too.

Darren was still with me. He had made it clear he was not going anywhere and I was still dressed in my day clothes when a theatre nurse arrived dressed in scrubs. She said she had come to fetch me but was surprised I wasn't yet wearing my surgical gown. It was 10am and she handed me a gown and let me get ready by drawing the curtain around me. Suddenly, my hands were like jelly and I felt a little panicked as I stripped off to put on the gown. Darren kept saying, "Other way round," and I was saying "No, they go on like this." The nurse came back and started to laugh and told me that I had it on the wrong way round. Typical. Darren had been right. So, here I was, covered in marker pen, naked apart from a pair of paper pants (hospital issue, not my own, you understand), ridiculously tight navy stockings that cut in at the knee and a gown that I didn't even know if I had the right way up let alone the right way round. She kindly sorted me out and it occurred to me that there was no point getting precious about how I looked as they were all going to see it soon anyway.

I put my slippers on and was just about to follow her when she asked where I was going, "With you?"

"You aren't walking," she said.

I had to get onto my bed to be wheeled down to theatre. This was embarrassing. I half lay, half sat, feeling like a fraud as the porter released the brake on my bed. I caught the lady opposite looking at me and she gave me the thumbs up calling, "Courage!" and I replied, "And a smile."

When I think about that day, I often think about her. I hope and pray she is still fit and well, talking about her daughters and passing wind without a hint of embarrassment. She took the time to encourage a complete stranger who was white with fear and her words struck a chord with me. Cancer is a funny thing, in many ways it picks on the strong, and that morning, she was my star and she guided me through a difficult time. She made me laugh but, most of all, she gave me the reassurance that I dearly needed. If she could do it, then I had no excuse, I could do it too. (Thank you Special Lady x)

I was then wheeled along the corridor with Darren walking on one side and the breast care nurse walking on the other as she had to officially hand me over to the theatre team. We then went through the double doors marked "Theatre" and my smiling team were sitting waiting for me. I recited my name, date of birth and the official handover was made. So, with my twisted gown, sexy stockings and glasses, which I needed to keep on until the last minute or I wouldn't see anything, I had to say my goodbyes to Darren. All a little bit public but he came round to my side, kissed me, gave me his knowing smile and then had to leave.

As my bed was turned and wheeled away, Darren stood and waved and one of the nurses remarked, "How lovely."

"What?" I asked, "He's off to the restaurant for a cooked breakfast!"

They all laughed, but I added, "He is lovely though." Then a thought went through my head – would this be the last thing I said? What were Darren and I doing wasting all this time by not being happy and now it could be too late? Had I missed my chance of being happy because of this squatter in my breast? Was I ever going to be someone's wife again? Would I ever get to live the fairy tale? Now it was just me and the squatter that were being wheeled through another set of doors and I was praying that only one of us came out of theatre. But I knew what was waiting for me on the other side of the doors. It was time for Operation Clare!

CHAPTER 9 – ANGEL IN SCRUBS

As I was wheeled through the double doors into the Anaesthetic Room, I saw my surgeon in his scrubs standing in the corridor by the window smiling at me, "See you soon," he said. I smiled back and replied "Yes you will." It occurred to me that it was such a nice, yet simple thing to say, and it was encouraging that he genuinely cared so much. He was treating me like we knew each other so well and showed real empathy.

I found myself in a small area where I was transferred from one bed to another. It was the usual thing, me trying to do it in one swift energetic movement while trying to hold onto a little bit of dignity by holding my gown together, wearing surgical stockings and tearable paper pants. The result? A big ridiculous elephant trying to do a scissor jump from one bed to another! Another short journey into yet another room where I met "Mr. Mallet The Anaesthetist." Two nurses helped me sit up and a variety of pads were stuck all over my back. As I glanced to the floor I could see a bag with someone's lunch poking out the top, "Mmm, who do the crisps belong to?" I asked. The nurse laughed and said, "That's my bag! Are you hungry?"

"Starving" I said. We starting chatting about the joys of a packet of crisps and I joked about why had I gone through all this to be anaesthetised in a staff canteen? I lay back down, still thinking of crisps (no breakfast, remember) and a young trainee nurse was told to put the catheter into the back of my hand. She looked nervously to the senior nurse for reassurance and asked if she was hurting me. "No, I couldn't feel a thing" was my reply, "You did very well."

Mr Mallet continued the conversation on crisps as he had my anaesthetic ready, "You will only feel a slight scratch," he said. Why, oh why do they say that? "You will only feel like I am jabbing a great big knitting needle through your skin" would be more accurate. He asked what flavour crisps I liked and I waxed lyrical on my favourite subject, and something of which I am an expert, "Well, I do like bacon flavour." He told me to lie back, relax and just look at the ceiling while I continued talking, "I can feel my arms tingling," I said, "But, I also like…"

Gone! No crisps, no consciousness. I was under. Then, what seemed like minutes later, I could hear someone softly saying my name. I opened my eyes and saw a smiling nurse. I was in the recovery room. I focussed on her face and gave a wonky smile in response. She asked if I was in any pain and I had to concentrate on that for a moment before replying as I was still feeling quite light-headed.

"Only slightly," I said.

She gave me some paracetamol and my first glass of water.

"What time is it?" I asked and she laughed.

"Why, do you have to be somewhere?"

"Darren and my family won't know where I am."

"He's on his way down," she said, stemming her laughter.

Ridiculous, I know. It was hardly likely that Darren and my family didn't know where I was! "Have you seen Clare?" "Nope, you?" But my concern was more that they would be worried and I wanted them to know at the earliest opportunity that I was out of surgery. It was 2pm. My real concern should have been with myself and the fact that I had just undergone major cancer surgery, but I was still half out of it and as usual my priority worrying about everyone else.

I suddenly realised that I had my glasses on and its case was lying next to me as I was tucked very neatly into my bed. How thoughtful! Someone had popped my glasses on so that I could see when I woke up. It's not that I expected to wake up half-blind, gown wide open with everything hanging out and paper pants all askew, but still, they had tucked me up in bed like a small child. It was warming to think that even when you're completely out of it, they still treat you with the utmost respect.

I wasn't the only one in the recovery room, and there were other bleary-eyed figures trying to focus on their surroundings. As I glanced over to the door, there was my Angel in Scrubs. My Surgeon. He came over, took my hand gently in his and asked how I was feeling.

"OK," I said.

"It was a success," he said, "I think we've got it all."

"Thank you so much," I replied. The pain I was in no longer

—

mattered to hear those words.

"I will see you later," he said and he made to leave.

I struggled to let go of his hand and squeezed it, just a little bit longer. How could I let this man go? This wonderful, thoughtful, talented man.

My nurses arrived to wheel me out when one said, "Look who's coming." No, not Gerard Butler, who had finally realised that I was the girl for him, but Darren, grinning from ear to ear. I was still a bit dazed and then I was wheeled back onto the ward, glad it was all over and glad I was in one piece. I was put on oxygen and drifted in and out of sleep. I didn't feel nauseous thankfully, but felt woozy and drunk, without the booze of course, on morphine. Darren sat next to me the whole time reading his book. The nurses allowed him to stay there all day and each time I came round it was settling to see him there, momentarily, before I drifted back off into a drug induced haze. Every so often he would plump my pillows and pass me small cups of water, saying the odd comforting words before I drifted off again, as I was increasing the intake of oxygen at any given chance. No one asked him to leave, and anyway, he wasn't leaving alone, we would be leaving together. He wasn't going to leave Bear on her own in a time of crisis. He was a credit to the nursing profession, running around servicing my demands! He saved them a huge job. With the cancer gone all I had to concentrate on now was recovering.

At around 4pm, I was coming to a bit more when I saw another patient wheeled back in to the ward. She was not well and kept being sick into her hand-held grey cardboard bowl, but one thing I did notice was that she was wearing her pyjamas.

"I want my pyjamas on," I said to Darren in the manner of a spoiled child but still pretty much out of it.

"Bear, you need to stay as you are," he replied, with the twisted gown, paper pants and sexy surgical socks on, (me, not him!).

Like a mardy child, I said again, "I want my pyjamas on. She's got hers on!" I said in my best drug induced voice! Even if she did whiff of vomit, she looked prettier than me in her pyjamas. I was still wearing my iodine soaked gown and no part of me felt pretty. I was stripped of my femininity and wanted anything that would make me feel female again.

I had bought my pyjamas especially for this hospital stay and the least they could do was to let me retain a little dignity as I hobbled to the loo in the middle of the night with my bare bottom securely hidden in my specially purchased pyjamas. So, Darren dutifully got them out and pulled the curtain around my bed. First, we removed my gown, which immediately exposed the drain bottle which, at this point, was not secreted away in a nice flowery shoulder bag. Darren helped me get into my front-buttoned pyjama top which was remarkably easy.

Next, it was the turn of the pyjama bottoms. OK, not as easy, but hey, I've put pyjama bottoms on before, how hard can it be? I was still determined to get these things on despite still being slightly off my face with drugs and Darren was chewing his lip working out a plan of action. It was all going well until I thought it would be a good idea to lean back on my elbows and heave myself up the bed. Wrong! Pain? Yes! It seared through my entire body and I experienced flashes before my eyes. I was on the verge of passing out and puking all over my especially purchased pretty pyjamas. Darren dropped everything and dashed off to get a grey cardboard bowl for me to vomit into, the colour of which bore an uncanny resemblance to the colour of my face. Sweat was pouring out of every pore and I just put my head back on the pillow. He came running back in with the bowl as he was explaining to the nurse what I had done.

"Sod the bottoms!" I said to them both as I inhaled more oxygen, conked out and drifted back off to sleep.

Throughout being in and out of consciousness, my blood pressure was taken regularly to ensure everything was as it should be and then they brought my evening meal. In the morning, with no breakfast, lasagne with broccoli had sounded delicious…now? I ate it really slowly, not really tasting it, and my private nurse, Darren, sat at the side of me helping me with every movement.

Sadly, the lady on the ward who had taught me how to be strong had gone home. It was sad that I wouldn't see her again. She had made me laugh hysterically, but had also given me the courage to get through possibly the hardest day of my life. It was just me and one other patient on the ward now.

I was still struggling through my sea of lasagne when my Angel in Scrubs appeared. "Haven't you gone home yet?" I asked him. "Leaving soon," he said. He perched on the edge of the bed and explained that during surgery he had removed the tumour and had looked at it under a microscope. The decision was that more tissue had to be taken which is why the operation was extended but until he had a full report from Histology (cell examination) we wouldn't know the grade and stage of the tumour and if my margin was clear, but he was already pretty certain. As per protocol, the margin around a tumour has to be between 2mm and 5mm for it to be classed as clear. Only ten days to wait, but that would give me valuable recovery time.

A nurse told me that I could go home that evening, if I wanted to, but I felt far from ready and begged Darren not to take me. "You aren't going home," he said. I did not feel like the anaesthetic was out of my system and if I took ill it was a Friday night and I would be 20 miles from the hospital. The sick pyjama lady on the other side of the ward was leaving and as she was wheeled out she hollered to me, "Right or wrong, I'm going home. Take care." I replied with, "I'm not going!"

It was 8pm and Darren was exhausted. I had been asleep most of the day, but he had been up with me since 5am that morning and had gone through the trauma of sitting waiting for me in surgery, eating his cooked breakfast and sitting by the side of the bed, while I drifted in and out of consciousness making ridiculous demands, making him run around looking for cardboard sick bowls. He had only left my side to make reassuring telephone calls to family. Tom had decided that he didn't want to visit me in hospital, as he could not bear to see me that way. It was difficult enough for him to cope with what I was going through and not seeing the reality helped him. Darren gave me a kiss goodnight and said he would see me in the morning after a good night's sleep, as I settled back to read my book.

Another patient had arrived on the ward and she pestered the nurses all night with her bell. She was a complete nuisance and when one of the nurses had seen to her for the hundredth time, I asked what time lights out was. She laughed and said I made it sound like a prison, (funny that), but it was 10pm. I thought it would be a good idea to pop to the loo before everyone settled down and she said that she would need to come with me. She adjusted the bed, held my drainage bottle, and I swung my legs round so my feet touched the floor. I instantly felt weak and wobbly, and we slowly, really slowly, shuffled down to the toilet. The nurse, my drainage bottle and me could not all get through the door at once, so we had to shuffle in sideways, then she gently lowered me down to the toilet seat and I laughed at how I felt like a child. The three of us then shuffled like a three-legged race over to the sink then back to my bed which seemed like miles away. She tucked me in, made sure I was comfortable, closed my curtains around me and whispered, "Would you like a cup of tea?" Oh, the care of these people was never-ending. A brew? Nectar of the gods! It was the best cup of tea I had ever had.

Eventually, after a busy day sleeping, you know how it is, I turned off my reading lamp expecting a good night's sleep. I was disturbed continuously not by my pain but by the pain on the other side of the ward continually calling for attention. I was also woken to have my blood pressure taken, but really, it took seconds to drift back off. I also took the opportunity to pop a few pain relief pills as the drugs trolley wouldn't appear until 6am and my anaesthetic was starting to wear off!

CHAPTER 10 – TIT FOR TAT

The next morning, after my disturbed night's sleep, I was sitting up in bed preparing to take myself for an old lady wee. A nurse assisted me as I got out of bed and we slowly shuffled down the corridor to the toilet. This time I was allowed to go in on my own, as she felt I was doing so well and every achievement counted. I didn't feel like I was doing so well as it felt like I was in slow motion.

I made it back to my bed, placed my breakfast order and the bed makers arrived. So gutted! I was really looking forward to settling myself back into my bed and, as I was going home, it didn't seem fair to wreck a perfectly made bed with sharp corners on the sheets. I managed to get dressed with one arm, (well, when I say "dressed," I pulled on some jogging bottoms, socks and a fleece over my pyjama top, but another achievement) collected my toiletries and shuffled back down to the bathroom. Isn't it amazing how much better you feel after a warm wash? I always wanted to marry the man who invented the shower! Presuming it was a man? I went back to my bed and sat reading until breakfast arrived. I was relieved that I was going to be eating alone. The squatter was evicted!

A breast care nurse came and introduced herself and wanted to check how I felt and to change my dressings. She drew the curtains around the bed and I sat facing her when she removed the dressing and asked me to look down. Apparently, part of the recovery process is for you to see what has happened and accept it and I thought that it couldn't be so bad as I wasn't in any pain, just a little discomfort. I looked down to see a misshapen, partly blue from the dye, bloodied badly multi-coloured bruised breast and gasped.

At first glance it looked like there was a whole chunk of me missing, "It's fine," she said, "Once the bruising has gone down it will be fine." She could see the look of horror on my face as I then took a closer look at the drainage pipe sticking out the side of me! What the...? She gave me the pretty flowery shoulder bag that it fitted neatly into, but I hadn't prepared myself for where the tube would be. I didn't remember signing up for any of that!

We discussed my pain relief, which came in a big paper bag like a takeaway, and we put a date in the diary for my drain removal. Nice! She continually reassured me that everything was going to be OK as I'm pretty sure the look of horror had not yet faded from my face. I think I had returned to my cardboard grey colour. With all this information spinning in my head, Darren arrived and was surprised to see me sitting up and dressed with my bag packed. Don't get me wrong, it wasn't that I was so desperate to get home – I may have just had major surgery and found the hospital staff to be caring and attentive, but the usual organised Clare was obviously not affected by the anaesthetic, and let's face it, there wasn't much else to do. I received my discharge letter and headed for home.

Darren took my bag and we slowly walked towards the doors thanking all the staff on my way out. The corridors were endless and it seemed miles to the car, but it was good to stretch my legs again and be vertical for a while! Darren carefully placed me, and my trusty drainage bag, into the passenger seat. My strength had drained, likely into the flowery bag! A huge sigh of relief after all I had been through over the last twenty four hours, which in many ways seemed like five minutes ago, and I was looking forward to the comfort of my own home.

The journey was reasonably smooth as Darren stuck to the motorway to reduce the amount of braking and accelerating which may aggravate the discomfort, and within half an hour we pulled onto my drive. He helped me swing my legs out of the car so my feet could touch the drive and then it was a gentle heave, in one slow but careful action, to get me to my feet without putting any pressure on my left side.

Another short shuffle up the path to the front door and then onto lovely soft carpet. Yay! I'd done it with no drama! He took me into the lounge and helped me change back into my pyjamas, (yes, the very ones!) lowering me gently into the armchair, my own soft pillow behind my head and a stool to put my feet on. Heavenly! I was still wearing the surgical stockings mind. Not my choice but advice from the hospital.

I was warm, comfortable, tired and so, so happy to be back at home, leaving the ghastly cancer back in the hospital and out of me. My squatter was finally evicted!

I drifted in and out of sleep when Tracey, her husband and my boy Tom arrived. Tom came straight over and perched gently on the arm of the chair and then put a tender, protective arm around me. It was a remarkable moment, all at once he was my baby boy who had been through all sorts of unknown fears about me, the boy I needed to protect, and yet, for the first time, I felt completely protected by him. That one simple gesture marked a moment of complete role reversal, he was taking over, making suggestions of things to be done and who was doing what as I sat weakly in the chair.

Darren was scurrying in out and out of the kitchen with mugs of tea, glasses of water and this was just the beginning. Over the next few days he was visiting the supermarket daily, arriving home with a carrier bag of comfort food, I didn't know one person could carry so many bags and in one hand! All that was lacking was an apron and a lacy hat as he acted as my personal maid, fetching and carrying anything I wanted. Well, I was the invalid remember!

Personal hygiene was to be the next event. How can one shower whilst having a drain attached to your body? Only one thing for it. Darren would have to hose me down in the shower. Not an ideal scenario for me as my personal hygiene is exactly that. Personal. But I had no choice, it was just tit for tat. He would help me undress and not very elegantly I would step into the shower. He would lather up the shower gel on a flannel and hand it to me to wash areas! He would then hose me down. I felt like a child. Since I couldn't bend, he would turn me around and wash all down the back of me and my legs. At one point making the comment that he must remember to get some truck wash!! I would then step out and he would pat me dry, but the best to come, he would blow dry me with the hair-dryer as there were areas he dared not touch! One amazing feeling! Clean pyjamas on and I was back to my poorly chair.

My appetite had diminished, but he made me eat healthily, little and often to regain my strength and the comfort of being at home ensured that I had no trouble drifting back off to sleep throughout the days. Like a cat, my body had shut down to sleep mode to aid my recovery. Each day, I would say to myself, "Tomorrow I will feel a little bit better" and every day, I did!

CHAPTER 11 – RECOVERY MODE

Before I knew it, it was time to return to the hospital to have the "Redivac" drain removed. Not exactly a great day out, but Darren and I took the usual journey back to the hospital and were shown into a side room. The nurse removed both the dressing and the stitch that held the drain in place, and then released the suction from which I felt a tiny kick-back but nothing too extreme. She explained that I needed to take a deep breath in and that as I breathed out, she would remove the tube. She told me that it would be uncomfortable and described it as feeling like untangling wool inside me. I held onto Darren's hand, tightly, expecting the worse, but it was suddenly over.

They both stood looking at my wound, almost as if it wasn't part of me, saying what a good job the surgeon had done. She told me to look in the mirror at my breast and I suppose this was still part of the recovery process. As I turned to look, all I could see was yellow and black bruising and dried blood. That was it, I was going to hit the deck, blood was rushing to my feet, away from my head, and I could see stars and various other shiny things! I was not good looking at things like this at the best of times, least of all on myself. Darren picked up the closest thing to hand to waft a breeze into my face, which turned out to be a surgical metal tray. He apologised to the nurse that this may not the best thing to use, but she was halfway out the door to get me a glass of water. I sat for a few minutes to recover myself, a little embarrassed that I was being so squeamish, and then got dressed to leave. It was much easier now that I had the freedom of movement back without the drain.

Back at home, I was still in recovery, still being the invalid and unable to do housework. But, within the week I was back at my desk, logging back into the real world that had carried on without me, and checking emails to try and get back into my work and normality.

During that week, my mum and Sarah planned to visit. Sarah and I had not spoken for a couple of years due to a family dispute, but she was driving my mum to see me and I felt that as they had a three hour journey it would be ridiculous for her to drop my mum at the door and disappear for a few hours until she picked my mum up again. Certain events in your life give you a whole new perspective on things, which at the time seem important, and then suddenly pale into insignificance. Let's face it, I had just experienced one truly huge event, so some petty squabble over something which neither of us could remember any more, it seemed pointless to let it continue.

My mum rang to let me know what time they were arriving, and I felt it was time to draw a line in the sand and move on, so I suggested that Sarah came in with her. My mum appeared at the front door with a bagful of goodies, biscuits, magazines, flowers, and I gave her a one-sided hug. Then Sarah walked up the drive, also laden down with more bags of goodies and as she came closer I put out my right arm to give her a hug and it was gently returned. There was nothing to say, no old disagreements to discuss, we had moved on to a new chapter in our lives. We were sisters, we loved each other, and we had been through enough.

I followed them both as they went through to the kitchen as all sorts of things were taken from the bags. Everything was there, even Christmas crackers! As it was only mid-October, I think my mum feared I would not be able to do my Christmas shopping! We sat and had a cup of tea and then some lunch. Darren had left prior to their arrival as he felt that we needed to be on our own, and possibly to also give himself a well-earned break.

A short time later, Tom got back from school. We saw him pass the window on his bicycle as he headed to the garage to put it away. Sarah had a last minute panic wondering if he would be OK with them being there as they had not seen him in the past two years. The door opened and he stepped into the room. There was a split second pause as everyone waited for a reaction, but he smiled and asked if everyone was all right. Simple! Easy! No complications! That's Tom. They couldn't believe the change in him, particularly now that he was taller than all of us and had a really deep voice. My mum stood up and walked over to give him a hug and then Sarah stood up and asked if she could have a hug too. Everything was OK, and Tom sat down and answered a thousand and one questions about Sixth Form, football, football and football!

Time flew by and it was around 9pm when they had to leave for their three hour journey home. I didn't want them to leave and they were reluctant to go too. None of us had expected that they would stay this long, but their main concern was that their delay meant that I had not had any rest that day. I was still on a high that everything had gone so well, and they were back in my life, and I knew there was plenty of time to catch up on sleep. Just after I'd waved them off until they disappeared around the corner, Darren rang to say he was on his way back.

Over the following days I just got better and better and Darren could not believe my healing qualities. I was quite surprised too; it was amazing what the body can do when it needs to step up to the mark. There was no infection, no swelling and both the doctors and nurses said I was recovering well. I discovered that a lot of it was a case of mind over matter If you think positively enough, despite all the stress that you are putting your body through, the recovery seems to speed up. You have to listen to the advice, your body and do nothing but concentrate on recovering.

Another week passed, and it was time to start my recovery exercises. The hospital provided me with a DVD to follow and it started easy enough, until I got to week two. I stood against the lounge door and had to raise my left arm as far as I could. I was now, mentally, in a different place with my body and it was almost as if I could sense every movement, every twinge, and every pain. As I lifted my arm it felt like I could feel every tendon being stretched within an inch of its life. This is called "cording." Whereas I thought this DVD was simple, already by week two I could only get my arm to 90 degrees. I was gutted. Maybe I didn't have such a miraculous healing ability, and I already doubted that I would ever be able to get my arm any higher. My independent spirit took another blow – all the years of cleaning my own house and car, all my gardening, all my decorating – my life was now going to be so restricted. Would I have to hug my son with one arm from now on? Would I be able to pick up my future grandchildren easily? All of these things were racing through my mind because cancer had thought to change something in my life without asking.

Only a few hours of feeling sorry for myself before determination kicked in again and over the following days, I managed to lift my arm higher and higher. Again, the importance of thinking positive. By week six, I could extend my arm so that I could point to the ceiling. If I told you it took me six weeks to point at the ceiling it doesn't mean a lot when you're fit and healthy, but for me it was an enormous achievement. I was forever sliding my arm up the wall and standing straight against it to get it stretched out. A word of advice – trust the medics and follow their advice, particularly when you start to doubt yourself! Every day, in every way, you will just get better and better, but a part of your recovery is that you have to help yourself. Not all of it, I grant you, but positive thinking is a powerful drug and not available over the counter!

On 24th October 2011, I returned to see my surgeon at Glenfield for my results. I was pleased, and proud, of my progress with the exercises and was looking forward to him complimenting me on my wound healing and brilliant recovery mode. My scar looked amazing, a narrow pink line which was hardly noticeable. As usual, I gowned up, admittedly badly, and he examined me saying how pleased he was, then he delivered the results of my surgery.

My "clear margin" around the tumour was not as clear as they had hoped it would be. The protocol requested a margin of between 2-5mm and the area at the top of my tumour was only 1mm. I had been remarkably high and positive when I'd first arrived, almost weirdly excited that he would be so pleased with my progress. I was buzzing but now I was back to being shattered as he toyed with the idea of more surgery. However, the surgery could not be done immediately, but he explained that this disease can take it upon itself to spread very quickly and as they were not sure if any of the cancerous cells had jumped the borders of the margin, chemotherapy was to be the next immediate stage. The length of time I would need to wait for further surgery was too long and too risky in case the aggressive cancer started to spread. I could not be left without any imminent treatment. Then came another blow, my surgeon was due to retire and would not see me through to the end of my treatment. He was going to pass me on to another surgeon who would then decide on any future procedures.

I felt completely panic stricken. Not only had I been relying on this man to save my life, but he was familiar with my case, with what was going on inside me and he always knew what needed to be done. He kept weighing up the pros and cons of further surgery and could not seem to make up his mind. What I really wanted him to say was, "Look, as I'm so familiar with all this, I will delay my much needed retirement and become your personal surgeon." I don't know if the nurse could read the look on my face, or perhaps I had said my thoughts out loud, unlike me, but she assured me that the future surgeon would know everything there was to know about my particular case, and it would be as if he had performed the initial surgery himself.

The oncologist was on site in the main hospital and the surgeon suggested I go to see him to arrange the chemotherapy. It would just be speeding the process up. I knew then it was a tearful gentle goodbye, and I thanked him for everything he had done for me. I told him I wished him well for his retirement, still secretly hoping he would change his mind, and like at the hospital I did not want to let him go. I took a little comfort when the nurse told me that he was not totally happy leaving my breast cancer case as I was one of his last patients and, I suppose, he had to stop somewhere.

I got dressed and was handed my records, which was now a good thick folder of notes which Darren had to carry, to see the oncologist. While I waited, it suddenly started to become all too real to me about what was happening and I was heading back into that dark place. We all hear about chemotherapy, we may even know someone who knows someone who's had it. We may not understand it, but we know it's not something anyone would particularly want to have. I felt like I was opting for a lethal injection. It's not even a very nice word. Suddenly, a new emotion was starting to take a grip, terror. I started talking rapidly, my voice thick with emotion and Darren saying what he could to reassure me. I was falling to pieces in the waiting room. I had now lost control of this bad situation and I was in tears. This was another day with a totally different turnout than expected.

I heard my name being called and I went in to meet the oncologist. He had only briefly read through my notes a few minutes before and as I put on yet another gown, he examined me. There was no small talk and he came straight to the point when I asked him about hair loss. He mentioned a "cold cap," which is basically a frozen helmet that freezes your hair follicles to help reduce hair loss before, during and after chemotherapy. Brain freeze, quite frankly! He didn't seem very enthusiastic at its ability to work and told me that it was pretty inevitable that I would lose my hair. He told me that I had aggressive cancer and he needed to treat it aggressively. Fair enough! Not exactly fluffy bedside manner, but perhaps it was what I needed to hear right then. He went on to explain that I did not need any preventatives in my body as the chemotherapy needed to spread everywhere, not just 90% of my body, and potentially the cold cap would prevent it getting to the very top of my head.

I hadn't really prepared myself for this meeting, so I was struggling to ask, and answer questions. In between sobs, it was arranged that I would have an appointment with the specialist nurse who would go through the details of the treatment in the Chemotherapy Suite. This date was to be the 3rd November 2011 and I would be back in their hands again. I had to increase my recovery mode and needed more help than ever!

CHAPTER 12 – THE RINSE CYCLE

The 3rd November 2011 soon came round. This appointment for oncology was to be at Leicester Royal Infirmary rather than Glenfield Hospital and the reality of all this was settling in again. Darren and I arrived and the sign above my head in the corridor directed us to the Osborne Building for the Chemotherapy Suite, the one choice that everyone would rather avoid. As we entered the department I was back in that exclusive cancer club again, a fully paid up member with honours. Headscarves and wigs were on display, examples on how to wear the various styles of headscarves, wigs in blonde, brunette, flowing locks and neat bobbed hairstyles, all depending on your mood.

I wasn't in the mood as it happened and walked swiftly past as if to deny that I needed any of these options. We went through some double doors and the first thing I saw to my left was a row of patients all sitting in armchairs hooked up to drips, either sitting chatting to nurses or reading and eating. What the heck am I doing here? I feel fine, really, can I go now?

I was standing at reception, pretty dumbstruck, and handed over my appointment letter. There didn't seem to be many patients waiting in there so I thought this was a good omen. The receptionist scored through my name on a list in a bright pink highlighter pen and requested that I take a seat in a waiting room a little further on. So this was where everyone was, and the room was packed. Take what seat? People were standing, there were bald women reading magazines, women with headscarves, some wearing a single glove, didn't know what that was about. It wasn't just restricted to women, there were men waiting for their appointments too. I felt like a complete fraud, I didn't belong in there, I was fit and well, I had my hair, I had my boobs, but I had no seat! There were nurses and medics flying in and out of various rooms, everyone was busy. Naturally, we were standing in everybody's way when a nurse came over and suggested that we walked further down to a day room, and as they knew how busy they were, there was no worry over not being able to hear my name being called as they would come looking for me. That's a shame! I was more than keen on not being found.

The day room had chairs but no air conditioning and it was hot, really hot. I waited for a very long half hour when I heard my name being called. We followed a nurse into a private room and she had a trainee with her and after being asked, I assured her that I didn't mind her staying. An array of forms was placed on the table, which indicated to me that this was going to be a long meeting. The specialist nurse then proceeded to explain chemotherapy, the rinse cycle, its pros and its cons. I don't think I immediately took in the pros and the cons which seemed to go on forever. She also indicated, which I thought oddly at this stage, that it was still my decision whether or not to go ahead. Like there's an option? My heart was screaming, "No, get out while you can. Run!" My head, my stupid sensible head was screaming back, "Of course you are going through with this, you crazy woman. Get that form signed and be quick about it!"

The nurse explained that the course of chemotherapy I was going to have was called FEC. This was strangely apt, as it was a word I used in my head quite a few times during the meeting! It actually stands for "fluorouracil epirubicin cyclophosphamide." Doesn't exactly trip off the tongue, no matter how many times you practise it, and I have. How impressive would that look, turning up to my allocated appointment and announcing loudly that I was here for my fluorouracil epirubicin cyclophosphamide! It occurred to me it was the sort of thing you might ask for at a garden centre when you were trying to get rid of a particularly stubborn weed, and in many ways, I suppose this is exactly what it was going to do!

I would be having six treatments of this combination and a nurse would administer it by injection rather than through an intravenous drip. It would take about an hour to inject the required dose into me and there would be seven "elephant" sized needles administered. The first one was to contain a bright pink liquid and she suggested I check the colour of my pee after this one. Incidentally, I did, and it's the pinkest pee I've ever had – just in case you were interested! It sounded all very "lethal injection" to me, why on earth would anyone go through all that by choice?

The courses would be three weeks apart, so the whole

—

treatment would take a total of four months. Each chemotherapy course also kills every white blood cell in the body, including the healthy ones, and the three week gap gives the body chance to recover and reproduce them. Then you go back and do it all again, another five times. It asks a lot from your body to take you through it each time, but that's what it's designed for I suppose. It takes them all out regardless. I have a history of anaemia but she assured me that this would be OK and then she gave me a list of dates and times for my treatment.

I asked her about sickness and what would happen if I wasn't well enough to attend a session. She told me that it was vital that I shouldn't vomit after a treatment, as this would remove the chemotherapy from my body before it had chance to do its work and it was very likely the vomiting would not cease. She then talked a bit more about the side effects – constipation was one. Great! This was an issue because it was important that you "get rid of the waste" chemo as "naturally" as possible as it can cause damage. She listed the food I couldn't eat, one of which was soft cheese. Isn't it odd what your subconscious does? Now I was banned from eating it, I suddenly had a burning desire to eat some! "What would you like for tea?," "Soft cheese please!"

We then started to talk about the area I really didn't want to think about or accept would happen – the hair loss! How the hell was I going to cope with losing my hair? What woman really can? The cancer was taking away my femininity and now it was going to take my hair! But, I had no choice. No damned choice at all. There was no more time for delay and I could not take time out to think about it. I was going to have to accept it. But it's still a conversation you do not want to have. Was I ever going to have any luck? I remember as a child being on holiday with Sarah and my mum at Lowestoft. We left our socks and shoes in the middle of the beach and ran down to the sea. As I looked back, I saw a Jack Russell dog approach my shoes and duly cock his leg. I spent the rest of the day in warm green socks and damp shoes!

So, was there the vague chance of possibly keeping my hair by looking again at the option of the cold cap? She explained that you wear a freezing helmet for one hour before the treatment and then wear it for a further two hours after the treatment. I considered that maybe putting those few hours aside every three weeks with a good book was perhaps an option and may not be as bad as I had been led to believe. She asked if I wanted to try one to see how I felt about it. I said, "OK" seeing a small window of something positive for a change and firmly believing that this was going to be a way of at least keeping my hair. She left the room and I chatted light-heartedly to the trainee, maybe things were looking up for a change?

She returned with a cool box that you would take on a picnic. She lifted the lid and took out what looked like a horse riding helmet made of a grey material. It was not a good look for anyone and she popped it on to my head, strapping it under my chin. Within seconds, I could feel the cold seeping into my head, it felt similar to ice cold water running on the inside of my head from the top of my scalp. It was remarkably heavy and I suddenly thought, with a sinking heart, "I'm not sure I could wear this." Already with the weight of it, I could feel my neck and shoulders not liking it either. Bit of a blow actually, but common sense kicked in, what was more important? Getting rid of the wretched cancer, or hanging onto my hair? Hair that given time, would grow back. I needed this chemotherapy to reach everywhere. Why would I go through this to receive less than 100% treatment? Out of all the sights I'd seen today in the waiting room, I had not seen anyone else wearing a cold cap, so I reluctantly took the advice the oncologist gave to me a few weeks ago, and rejected the idea. As I tore off the Velcro strap I reassured myself that I had good solid Irish roots to my hair, my grandfather had very thick dark hair, so it was in my genes and I needed to put aside my worries on that score and get on with getting rid of the cancer before it got rid of me.

The nurse then offered me something you aren't offered every day and it made me laugh out loud – I could have a free wig on the NHS! So, this is what I've been paying into the system for all these years! I told her very quickly that I could not do a wig, as I would be too clumsy with it. It would be like some awful comedy sketch and I would get out of the car leaving it on the back seat only to find that people had called the RSPCA because I hadn't left the window open to let in some fresh air. What if it was a windy day? What if I put it on back to front? I had enough pets as it was, I didn't need to walk around with one stuck on my head. This was all going to be bad enough without frightening small children and animals, and anyway, let's face it, I had glimpsed the ones on offer in reception, and I would look as if I was going to a very bad fancy dress party!

Instead, she gave me details of a cancer charity in Leicester called Coping with Cancer. Part of their service is a group of volunteers who work under the name Headstrong who would be able to advise me. She suggested I made an appointment to go and see them and they would show me how to take care of my scalp and explain how to tie headscarves properly so they don't come off every time you turn your head.

So, I had my dates, a head full of facts and still a full head of hair. I was to return in four days' time for my first treatment. Whoa wait a minute there! Four days? Well, this was it, no turning back now. I had the support, they had my details and I'd be back in four days' time for day one of my rinse cycle!

CHAPTER 13 – HAIR TODAY, GONE TOMORROW

Monday 7th November 2011 at 1.30pm was my first date with chemotherapy. What a joyous prior weekend that was! A strange set of nerves that I cannot explain. There's always that weight of something on your mind when you fall asleep, wake up, think about in the middle of washing up, waiting for the kettle to boil. Always there, nagging at the back of your mind. The feeling of panic was overriding everything and not knowing how I was going to be able to do this alone. I was scared and upset and was not afraid to say so. I had called the hospital to check that my blood test results were sufficient enough for me to be able to receive my first treatment and I told them that for my first session

I did not feel I could sit in the crowded room I had witnessed the first time I had visited the Chemotherapy Suite. They were their usual marvellous selves, and told me that they would ensure I was in a private room so that I was away from the noise and so that I could take my time to get used to what was going on. Tracey was going to be allowed to stay with me. Darren would be working and all would be fine.

When my escort Tracey arrived that morning, she remarked that I looked like a ghost. That was my face before I'd even started the procedure. I received supportive messages from family and friends and more advice from my friend who had been through all of this treatment a year before. We set off, reluctantly, for the Leicester Royal Infirmary Chemotherapy Suite, and I could think of a thousand other places I'd rather be. Through the main reception, passing the display wigs, I forced myself to have a closer look as I was still trying to convince myself to accept that I would be losing my hair. Onto the first floor and through the double doors to the suite, I handed over my still unmarked yellow appointment card, only to be told that the appointments were running an hour behind. Aaargh! No! I had planned in my head that I would be walking back out to the car by 3pm and that it would all be over. We had no option but to take a seat with the drinks, biscuits, fruit, soup and sandwiches all available to patients, alongside the copious, well-thumbed magazines. I had a drink and slowly ate my way through some biscuits to try and fill the nervous void that had appeared in my stomach. It was possible that they would make a re-appearance a little later, so I tried to choose the least offensive thing on the available menu, just in case.

There were nurses and medics everywhere, all scurrying up and down, in and out, all with something to do, some place to be.

There were orders being placed for chemotherapy cocktails, there were patients receiving their orders. Everywhere I looked in the waiting room was people in twos. It filled me with immense sadness as my eyes flicked from person to person, wondering who had the cancer, who was the victim, who was the willing supporter, wondering what cancer they had. It was a sorry sight. It wasn't fair. It was a sad place.

An hour later my name was called. I took a nice big swallow to reduce the possibility of seeing those biscuits sooner than I had predicted, as I was taken round to the main armchair seating area. I could feel my heart making me walk painfully slow, but my head taking over again and telling me to get my ass over there! There was a slight rise in my panic status, as I turned to the nurse and said in an unusually squeaky voice that I had been promised a private room. She told me to wait and came back with "No problem," and walked me over to a room just off the main suite. There was a man sitting in there hooked up to an intravenous drip and she explained that she was moving him. Crikey, I felt terrible, this was a terrible start. But he was charming and he smiled as he, and his drip trolley, was wheeled past me. We had eye contact and he kindly said, "I've warmed the seat." I thanked him and shakily walked over to the seat knowing that I wouldn't be leaving it until I was fully toxic!

As usual, the nurse was lovely, had obviously been in this situation before and knew how to gently handle a terrified patient. I desperately wanted to cry as the thought of this lethal injection just seemed wrong, but she constantly reassured me that she would take her time. She disappeared momentarily only to reappear with my drugs trolley. Wow! Seven huge vials of toxic FEC were to be entering my bloodstream. At no point in this journey had I even considered asking about the quantity that the chemotherapy would require, and here it was. Another rise of panic as I looked at the volume of liquid. and could not imagine it possible that my body could absorb this amount of fluid. It was the equivalent of giving someone seven pints of water to drink in one go. Now, beer I can do, but not this! Where was I going to put it all? I didn't even want to hold my hand out for her to begin.

She told me to relax whilst still explaining everything she was doing until I had to ask her to stop. The less I knew and imagined the better. I had to sit and watch the whole procedure and that alone was enough for me. She placed a pillow on my lap with a tissue lining under my hand. She then slowly rubbed my hand to get the vein to rise to the surface. Everything in me tensed, "please God no" a voice was screaming in my head, and I just wanted to pull my hand away and tell them all they had made a terrible mistake and I was fine, really, I didn't need this! But before I had chance to run for the door, there was my trusty vein. Big, fat and juicy and all ready for the nurse to plunge in a catheter and stick it down with plaster to the back of my hand. I'd told her I needed it to be white tape as I was allergic to the other plasters. I'm not allergic to many things, except plasters, oh and jellyfish stings which at that point seemed the better option, and as it seemed, hospitals now! She pulled the trolley closer to her, which was kitted out with drawers for more needles and cotton wool. She picked up the first FEC vial and checked the details written on the glass to ensure they tallied with me. Heaven forbid she should get the wrong inmate! Here was that voice in my head again, a little calmer this time, resigned to what was about to happen, "It's this or probable death Clare," it said "get on with it!"

Slowly, she started to administer the FEC which was freezing cold. I could feel the bright pink fluid slowly moving into the veins in my hand and creeping up my arm. I was rigid with fear.

My tongue was sticking in my dry mouth. I couldn't speak, unusual for me I know, as a vague paralysis had taken over so I couldn't move my arm or my hand which had gone into a cold sweat with fear. This was it, it had started! My life was literally in her hands.

She told me to tell her if I felt a burning sensation as this would mean that the chemotherapy had leaked into the tissues in my arm and bypassed the vein. It was really difficult to tell the difference between burning and freezing cold and I concentrated hard on what it was I was feeling. Suddenly, I had the overwhelming taste of metal at the back of my throat. It had hit the back of my nose and was like I had been sucking old coins or hit water hard. I could taste it everywhere and started to feel the need to gag. The metallic taste filled every part of my mouth and my saliva and it was unbearable. I needed mints, anything to take this taste away which was invading my nose and now my mouth. We talked continuously, partly through nerves, partly through trying to fill the ghastly silence where everyone would have clearly heard my heart thumping and that annoying screaming voice in my head whilst swallowing volumes of metallic saliva.

Tracey had the same panic-stricken look on her face, as I imagined I had, but she talked in a calm and soothing way, which helped. My admiration for the nurse was immense, what a job she had to do. Working with panic-stricken adults and worse, children with cancer. How must that be? Here I was, in my forties, but closer to my thirties just for clarification, and I was petrified. What must a child go through? She said that she did not see what she did as being particularly admirable, but I assured her it was. It far outweighed what she was doing for me.

I asked her why the other patients I had seen in the main room were hooked up to intravenous drips as they calmly read a book.

And my big question was why did they still have their hair? What was the deal? She explained that different cancers meant different treatments, and unfortunately, luck of the draw, my cancer and my treatment meant inevitable hair loss. I then asked her why I had seen some women wearing one glove and she explained that some ladies liked to wear a glove to keep their hand warm to ensure that the vein remain raised for the process, not because they are a Michael Jackson fan. That seemed sensible and straightforward until she added that, on occasion, the chemotherapy may have leaked out inside the hand and burned some of the tissue, which appears unsightly. Oh, dammit! Not all that pleased I'd asked!

Finally, my hour was over and I had finished my first session. She handed me a nice big paper bag of goodies from the pharmacy that I would need to take over the next few days. Three of them once a day, two of them throughout the day, one of them in the morning, two of these after eating! What? I wasn't taking any of this in so she kindly wrote all the instructions across the boxes. There was no room for error in taking these tablets. I had to get it right. I glanced at the pile of boxes and asked her if there were any for anti-nausea, "No," was her reply, but apart from the cold arm, I felt strangely OK, so we could go shopping after all. I was looking forward to my three weeks off before I had session two, my next appointment was made and I left the building, Elvis style!

We walked back to the car and rather than hopping and skipping across the tarmac, I walked tentatively, almost gliding so as not to pound my body, just in case. We drove to the retail park and I decided to stay in the car whilst Tracey popped out to do a bit of shopping. I was a bit conscious that I was toxic. I had messaged Darren at work to say all was OK and it had gone surprisingly well. At that my phone rang and it was my friend who had been guiding me through the treatments. She was ringing to ask how I had got on and when I told her that I felt fine, she warned me that I could feel nauseous later. But honestly, I was almost patting myself on my own back for feeling really quite well. It's a bit like that feeling you have of self-congratulation in the morning after a heavy night out when you feel remarkably well. It was not going to hit me, I really felt fine. She also mentioned that after her first session she had a "munchies" craving for burger and chips. Don't quite know what happened there, but with that suggestion I had the same craving! Tracey returned to the car and asked what we were doing for supper and I told her, without hesitation, "Chicken and chips!" It wasn't difficult to get her to agree!

By the time I got back home, I was still feeling great. I went to the toilet and had to call everyone in to look at my pink pee! Which of course, they did reluctantly. We watched TV and then we sent Tom out on his bicycle to get us our takeaway supper. Oh, yes! I could taste it! Yum! Couldn't wait! It was now about 7pm as he returned with chicken and chips. Mmm, the smell. I ate slowly and sensibly and then, you guessed it – a wave, a huge wave of nausea came crashing over me. I was drenched in sweat, it was all coming straight back up and I had to move fast. I clenched my teeth and ran to the kitchen and threw open the window to get some cold air. I felt terrible, awful, I was going to vomit, everywhere!

Tracey came rushing in after me and asked the obvious question, "Are you OK?" "God no," was all I could manage. I sipped some cold water and, although I hadn't actually been sick, we decided the best option for me was pyjamas and bed. I felt worse than I had ever felt before, and I could feel the colour draining from my now very sweaty face, almost like a cartoon character. I had not been given any anti-nausea tablets but I still had tablets to take as part of my new routine, so I took them through clenched teeth with more water. Tracey was staying overnight and I promised to call her if I needed to, but as I lay on my bed ten minutes later, after having another pink pee, waves of nausea rolling over me, that strong metallic taste filling my mouth again, the chicken doing the tango in my tummy and my bloodstream full of poisonous chemotherapy, it did occur to me that I never wanted to speak to anyone again because I had run out of adjectives on just how terrible I felt.

So this was it. This is what it felt like. I had started chemotherapy and I still had some way to go. I had my hair but how soon was it to come out? What if it was gone tomorrow? Maybe I'd try and remember this moment next time I craved chicken and chips! Goodnight!

CHAPTER 14 – MILK AND MAKE UP

Next morning I awoke and lay very still in bed. How did I feel? Oh no, I still felt nauseous! Wrong answer! How long was this going to last? I was also very conscious that I had a guest in the house, so I got up and Tracey came downstairs to ask how I felt, "Terrible," was my reply. This was like the worst hangover, ever!

Before I had my first chemotherapy session, I had been to visit my best friend's mum, who had just finished her bowel cancer treatment. Over a glass of wine, as you do, we discussed the treatment, how to deal with the sickness and so on. She had been a great help and had been open and honest, no holds barred, which was just what I needed. She was a very positive person, her usual smiling self and taught me how to deal with cancer head on. Even though we had different cancers, the treatments were very similar as were the side effects. I didn't want someone telling me, "Oh, you may feel a little queasy, but you will be fine and cart wheeling again in no time."

So, with this advice in mind I knew that I was going to be feeling nauseous for a few more days yet. She had also advised me of a make-up morning that was held at the hospital called "Look Good, Feel Better." It's a nationwide group of volunteer beauticians who come to the hospital once a month to teach you how to do your make-up so you look "normal" by filling your features back in. It's really aimed at how to disguise the loss of eyelashes and eyebrows during the chemotherapy treatment and to get some colour back into your face. Well known make-up companies donate products, along with perfume manufacturers, and you are given a complimentary bag of goodies, with a cup of tea and biscuit, while you chat to other patients. I had the number and booked my slot for the end of February, predicting I would not need it anyway.

I stood in front of the mirror and was shocked at the grey ashen woman looking back at me. I normally have a nice "swarthy" colour, as I've been described as such over the years, but this morning I genuinely looked ill. So, rather than wallow in self-pity, I washed and dressed to feel relatively human again, and then took my place in the "poorly" chair to watch daytime TV. This was my plan for the day, unless someone turned up and delivered me some work so I could try and take my mind off the waves of nausea I was still doing battle with.

I was still clinging to the fact that I had hair but had booked a hairdresser's appointment to have it cut from above my waist to a fairly short bob as I had been advised to do. This lessens the impact of the loss apparently, but I was, even now, still hoping that I would keep it. I also made an appointment for "Headstrong" at Leicester's "Coping with Cancer," where I'd learn scalp care and the best way to wear a headscarf or wig if one chose. It is another national group and these ladies were fabulous. When Darren and I arrived, we were ushered into a hot room and given a cup of very hot tea. Although I still had hair, they put a stocking on my head to hold my hair in place, then a scalp cap, then a headscarf. With all of that, the room was no cooler and I was losing weight in the heat! It may sound barmy, but I bought a few headscarves and a scalp cap, still believing I would not be requiring them but that I would have a few pretty scarves to wrap my hair into. Darren paid a donation to the ladies along with the purchase of my goodies and we left to get some cold, fresh air with our clothes still sticking to us.

Back at home on my poorly chair, I sat idly watching my cat Louis stretching out on his beanbag by the radiator. He was happy, warm and sleepy and I smiled to myself thinking how good it was that he would never have to feel as bad as I did. I was now in a constant state of mild panic and dread as I thought about what was going on in my body and that I had no way of controlling it. How did the chemicals know where to go and what to attack? Was the chemical damaging other organs? Was it doing irreparable damage to my liver, or had I already done that over a few girls' nights out?! What if it burns my heart or melts my bladder? Would the NHS take this into account and give me new ones? I would gladly take this pain for the cat and wouldn't want him to have to go through it. Clearly, he had become too warm and caught my eye. He slithered off the beanbag and stretched across the carpet towards pasty old me. Obviously he could sense that because of my blood cell reduction I was really cold, so rather than a warm cosy lap, I was the means for him to cool down. They say that animals can sense illness and sorrow, and that day he could sense it. He climbed up and settled down, to comfort me, to make everything all right again, and to cool down of course.

I had to eat, but everything that was put in front of me was like climbing a high mountain. I ate slowly, and cautiously, waiting for the moment it would all re-appear. Just the smell alone of cooked food was making me nauseous. Tom and I had always been big milk drinkers and I'd often considered cutting out the middle-man of the supermarket and just buying a big dairy cow to stand in the garden. But now, the thought of milk, the thought of that heavy creamy clotting liquid hitting the back of my throat was the worst thing ever. Instead, I was trying to do everything healthy, with a diet of fruit and vegetables. Little and often seemed to work better in keeping everything where it should be, but nothing seemed to be fighting the overwhelming feeling of exhaustion. My white blood cells were slowly being wiped out which left with me with very little energy and every movement was an effort. I drifted in and out of sleep, and this helped, because like a cat, if I shut down while I was poorly I wasn't awake to feel ill. Now, just in case you're reading this and thinking, "What's all the fuss? I've felt a bit sick before." This was continual, full-blown, teeth clenched, deep breaths, and cold sweat sickness. This was me telling myself over and over, "Don't be sick, don't be sick!" because I wasn't sure I would ever stop.

In preparation for the side effects, Darren had kindly bought me two large pink buckets. He thought the pink made it look more feminine and would represent breast cancer! One was decoratively put by my "poorly" chair, one was left by my bed, all very Feng Shui! I really hoped that I wouldn't be so ill that I'd have to use them, or worse, fill them!

The day didn't drag thankfully, and I knew that each day got me closer to my goal of feeling better. I didn't feel up to leaving the house, and I had done all the shopping, washing and cleaning prior to my treatment so I could relax with my feet up knowing that no-one would feel obliged to tackle a large basket of ironing on my behalf.

On the hour, my menu of "A La Carte" prescribed tablets were reluctantly swallowed, with steroids being the main course. Now, these little buggers gave me cravings like I'd experienced during pregnancy. They were prescribed to beat infection as I was very open and prone due to the treatment and surgery and worst of all, the weight gain. I had to keep myself clear of my dad due to his COPD condition as he regularly had chest infections. I could not afford to have any delay in my chemotherapy treatment as it had been confirmed that my margin around the tumour was not clear. This cancer had to go, not me! We had purchased anti-bacterial soaps and sprays and we were all very conscious of people coming in and out of the house and being around me. Hands were being constantly washed before entry to the kitchen. I was confined to the house. Friends were on hold for visiting, but they all understood. For the first seven days I seemed to be getting worse before getting better.

A supermarket own brand cheese flavoured crisp shaped into a ball! They were my first craving. Couldn't get enough of them. No other make would do and I found the strong artificial taste helped to disguise the overwhelming metallic taste I constantly had in my mouth. Darren came over in the morning and as soon as he'd walked through the door I told him, with urgency, that he had to go back out and get some for me as I had managed to polish off every packet I could find in the house. I was salivating at the thought of them. "Is he back yet?" I wondered, as I watched him pull off the drive!

When he got back I was in my "poorly" chair with a bowl ready for my first junkie hit! Then he broke the news, he'd been to a different supermarket instead, "Puffs, they're the same aren't they?" No they are not. They are a totally different crisp. The name "ball" and "puff" bears no resemblance. A moment of calm before the storm and then, "What? Tell me you are kidding?" I said ungratefully. No one would ever understand the importance of this particular snack food at this point in my life and as he poured this poor substitute into my bowl, I let out a sigh and thought that I may as well eat them as nothing. So, I did, and sulked all the way through them! I was just praying that someone would ring and ask if I wanted anything from the other supermarket!

After a night-time snack of more tablets I was off to bed, hoping that although I had drifted throughout the day I would be able to get a decent night's sleep. Darren had returned to work with his mobile on standby and Tracey was doing the night shift with me, neither of us sure if I was going to be fine or if I would need my pink bucket! I crawled into bed, shut my eyes and heard nothing...until 1.30am! My mobile phone was ringing and I could see it was a Coventry number. My first thought was that my dad must have been rushed to hospital and I sat up trying to get rid of the sleepy voice.

"Is that Clare Collins?"

"Yes" I replied in my pretend wide awake voice. The caller announced they were from an emergency vets in Coventry.

"Hello Clare. Do you own a cat called Louis?"

My mind went blank. Well, this wasn't the conversation I was expecting. I'd already raced ahead thinking that thankfully as Tracey was here she could go over to the hospital to my dad.

"Yes I do, why?"

"Unfortunately he has been hit by a supermarket lorry on the A5. A kind couple saw the incident and as it was 1am, they picked him up in a coat, placed him on the back seat of their car and drove him here."

My head was all over the place, but I asked, "How badly injured is he? Is he alive?"

"Yes," she said, "he has some damage to his front left leg but before we can treat him, we need you to come over to sign the forms of consent as the owner."

I was now completely awake and I said, "I'm 24 hours out of my first chemotherapy. I am not to go anywhere where there is likely to be infection. Can you treat him please and I will have to send someone over in the morning?"

"We can't I'm afraid. As the owner, we need you to sign the forms for treatment."

I was fighting cancer, this treatment had completely taken it out of me, and here I was having a conversation at 1.30am about going to Coventry to sign some paperwork in highly infectious surroundings. But then, it was Louis! My precious Louis, who not many hours ago had been sitting on my lap to comfort me. I got out of bed to write down the details of how I could find them and Tracey appeared, sleepily in the doorway, to ask what was going on. She too thought it was our dad, but when I came off the phone I told her what had happened. We were both shocked as we'd both assumed Louis was tucked up asleep in the conservatory. We went to get dressed and I was gulping back the sobs and the nausea because I knew I had to get there quickly to see my tiger cub. I had to be with him. Simple. Cancer can wait for the night! This supermarket was haunting me! Was this because I did not enjoy their version of flavoured crisps?

I woke Tom up to explain what was happening in case he came down to an empty house in the morning and panicked. Then Tracey drove us to Coventry. We found the centre reasonably quickly and the nurse let us in and told us to wait. I felt ghastly, tired, ill, and now upset about my poor Louis. The vet called us in and there was Louis, blood on his face, blood on his paws and my first instinct was to pick him up and hold him as he cried and I cried. All my cats are rescue cats and Louis had been poisoned at nine months old by his previous owners who had left him to die. As he convulsed they panicked and abandoned him at a vet. He was treated, fought back and re-homed to Tom and I in his forever home where he was loved.

Tracey was alarmed and said, "You can't be near infection." But it wasn't about me at that moment, and as I held him tight he stopped crying and he settled down. He is a beautiful animal, with a gorgeous nature and only deserves the best even though he can be quite timid. After all, like the rest of us, he didn't ask to be here.

I signed the treatment form and they gave him some morphine to ease the pain in his leg. I asked the nurse for some too, worth asking but didn't get any. She kindly told me that I could collect him later in the day. I gave him another kiss and a hug and sensed he wanted to come home with me, but, like me, he needed hospital treatment to make him better. We returned home and as I lay in bed worrying that I wouldn't be able to sleep now, I drifted off again. I telephoned the vets a few hours later and was told he was doing much better and had settled down. On this same morning I spent some time just looking in the mirror wondering what on earth I could do to make myself look half-human because I still looked terrible, but we drove back to Coventry to pick Louis up and we brought him back with a bag full of medication. The house was like a drugs den! We just had to make sure that we did not get our medication mixed up or I could have a bald cat craving supermarket cheese crisps!

So, not many hours before I'd been thinking how lucky he was not to be in any pain, and here we both were, full of medication, feeling sorry for ourselves. We were both wrapped up on the "poorly" chair, watching daytime TV, drifting in and out of sleep. Both had injection puncture marks on our paws. I was getting colder, then hot, then cold again. He was just warm and furry but slightly annoyed with the blanket being thrown off then put back on again.

Was I to spend the next four to five months of my chemotherapy treatment eating cheese flavoured crisps? It did not matter as I drank milk and applied make-up. Louis and I were there for each other and we would get better together.

I would tell myself, "Tomorrow I will feel a little bit better!"

CHAPTER 15 – KEEP IT UNDER YOUR HAT

Two weeks later, I was up for some retail therapy. I was feeling a lot better. I set off on my own to browse around the shops when I noticed the odd loose hair would drop down in front of my face. Thinking nothing of it I would just waft them away and continued in and out of shops. It was a chilly Saturday in November, I was all wrapped up and more and more hairs were dangling in front of my face like a spidery web landing on my scarf and coat. What's going on? I ran my hand through my hair in case there were any more loose ones and was left with a hand full of hair. Oh my God! It was happening! Here and now! My own worst nightmare, I was on my own, in a public place, and I was losing my hair.

I strode to the next shop, trying to keep a lid on my panic, and headed straight for the hats and hair bands. I needed to keep this hair on my head, at least until I made it home. I tried a headband on and it looked terrible, it didn't suit me at all, but now I had another dilemma. It was knitted and most of my hair was now stuck to it. I was still in the nightmare and it was getting worse. I needed to keep this hair in one place so I could make it to the car. I was panicking that it might just all fall out at once as it was evidently no longer attached to my scalp and it was now just resting on my head, waiting for a gust of wind to take it all in one go. Please don't let it be windy outside!

After I'd picked off as many hairs as I could, I threw the headband to the back of the rack, not maliciously, just out of horror of the situation I was in. I was in a wild panic. I found a headband that was a little wider, and walked to the counter to pay, having an out of body "I'm just having a bad dream" moment.

As I stood in the queue I was conscious of the people behind me. Were they looking at a large bald patch on the back of my head and pointing and laughing? I was shaking from head to toe, dry-mouthed in panic and my hands were sweating. The queue was taking forever, naturally, and I was moving from foot to foot, eager to pay and get the hell out. Why was it taking so long? Do I want a bag? What, for my head or the headband? I left the shop as quickly, and as carefully, as I could, not wanting to move my head too much in case the worst should happen. I got to the car and jumped in and needed to get home quickly. I dreaded looking in the mirror in case there were bald patches all over the place. There wasn't but I drove home crushed.

I dashed through the front door and immediately rang Darren.

God only knows what I was saying, I was just ranting, a few octaves higher than normal. This was all so bloody unfair. How could anyone love me when this was happening? How could anyone love me when I looked like this? All the insecurities I carried with me came tumbling out. My femininity was being taken away from me, cruelly and slowly to make it torturous, and I'd left some of it on the shop floor. He calmed me down and gently reminded me that we had been warned that this would happen. It still didn't make it right, and what I really wanted him to say was, "Don't worry, you won't lose any more."

Remember, this was two weeks in! Two bloody weeks! I knew I had worse to come and I didn't want it. Why couldn't this cancer just go and leave me alone? I didn't deserve this. What had I done that had been so bad? I had to stop the chemotherapy immediately as I couldn't go through with all this anymore. All of this was crushing me, I was quickly running out of the strength that everyone kept telling me would get me through all this. It was humiliating and degrading, and it was a dirty disease with a dirty name.

Darren had finished work so came over to see me. As we sat together I kept finding hair, everywhere. It was on the floor, on everything I had touched, on everything I had walked past, everywhere I had sat or stood in the house, there was hair. I even found some in my tea! What kind of horror film was this? I could touch my shoulder and have a handful of hair. I was beyond upset, gulping tears back, everything was now out of my control and I couldn't see any way of winning this fight. This cancer was going to kill me, no question. It was coming at me from every angle.

My eyes were stinging as I went to bed, emotionally exhausted, then I woke up in the morning and there was hair everywhere.

My pillow was covered in it. It was going on forever, every single hair falling, one by one, causing trauma. Don't forget, I had already decided to get it cut into a short bob, but a single piece of hair from the top of your head to the nape of your neck is still quite long. My sense of reason had gone, and I popped on a headband, stupidly thinking I could hang onto what hair I had left. But of course, this didn't work, it was still everywhere, and the last straw came when Darren hugged me and got it stuck to his face.

I was inconsolable and then Darren decided that maybe the best thing to do was to be proactive rather than reactive. He offered to get his brother's clippers and take off my hair before the cancer did. I ranted that it should be my decision, not the cancer's, and I didn't want to advertise my dilemma to everyone. It's not every Sunday afternoon that you borrow someone's clippers to shave off your girlfriend's hair because you want to be first in the race before cancer beats you at the finish line. It really felt like it was another battle I was losing in this war, and it was slowly overwhelming me.

Instead of going to his brother's house, Darren went out and bought some. As it was a Sunday, he left for the shops immediately because we could sort this out, once and for all. I reluctantly agreed and he returned with the box and left it on the table with no pressure. But I couldn't do it. I couldn't part with my hair. I'd already met the cancer halfway by getting my hair cut short, and now I had to openly admit how ill I was to everyone that would see me. It was torture and I was in hell. Today would be the day I would look like a stereotypical breast cancer patient and it broke my heart. I was supposed to be getting better, not worse. My hair appointment was set, Sunday 20th November 2011 at 3.50pm and Darren said that by 4pm it would all be over.

My hair would be gone.

This would be the next chapter in my woeful tale, and as he tried to console me by saying that I would still look beautiful without my hair, I ranted and cried, my face in my hands. If this was going happen, please let it be the worst part. This had to be the worst part. In comparison, the chemotherapy treatment suddenly didn't seem so bad. He led me to a chair in the middle of the kitchen floor and set up the clippers. I sat in the chair, hair still falling into my face before he'd even started. He slowly worked away, starting to shave above my right ear. It began to fall, slowly and gently into my lap and onto the floor. My beautiful thick hair was leaving me, but Darren was right there, supporting me through it.

Tom came through to the kitchen, and stood in the archway, silently watching. Louis followed him, curious to know what all the commotion was about, and hearing the familiar sound of clippers, possibly reminding him of having his leg shaved at the vets, was relieved that this time it was me and not him. The woman we all knew was slowly changing her appearance. Darren continued shaving the right hand side of my head and I asked Tom to pass me a mirror. I was back to my punk teenage days and suddenly had a thought that I hoped my head wasn't cone shaped! I checked in the mirror and there was a small bonus that my head was quite a nice shape, but I needed this to end as soon as possible. Darren slowly shaved the last bit and he saw that I was clutching a lock of hair.

"What are you doing with that?" he asked.

"I don't know," I replied.

"Put it in the bin Bear."

"I can't put my hair in the bin for the council to take. This is just so wrong."

He kissed the top of my head and regrettably, his face was covered in small pieces of my hair again. He had used a number one setting so I still had a dark covering on my scalp. That was a surprise and I wondered why I wasn't now completely bald. Oh no, had we just taken it all off when we really didn't need to? I was still in denial. I was not in a place I wanted to be. I was shifting my anger and frustration at cancer onto everyone around me. It didn't occur to me then, but a short time later, that as impossible and devastating this was for me, it was also difficult for those around me, for Darren who was cutting off his partner's hair. He could feel my degradation and was doing everything to make it better, but it was out of his control too. He told me to stand up and to shake off the hair that had fallen onto my shoulders, but not to look down and said, "Go and get a shower and put on one of your pretty scarves. When you come back down this will all be gone."

I did exactly as I was told and went straight upstairs. Hairs in a variety of all lengths stuck to my face by the hot tears and as I showered it just continued to come out. I patted my head dry and sat on the bed looking at my hair-dryer as it lay there, almost mocking me. Well, I won't be needing that, will I? I took out one of the scarves and put the small skull-cap on as I was already conscious how cold my head was. It took me almost 15 minutes to get the scarf right, on off on off, my arms were aching and the bow was finally straight. I looked in the mirror, carefully checking that you couldn't see any of the stubble on my head and that you couldn't see the white skull-cap, making sure it all covered my freezing ears. I moved my head from side to side to make sure it wouldn't come off and then looked closer. Looking back at me was a seriously ill woman with cancer! I barely recognised myself. I had reached promotion in the cancer club. I was officially wearing the uniform.

It was 6pm by the time I had stopped messing about and headed back downstairs and Darren, as promised, had completely cleaned the kitchen up. You would never have known that I had just lost my hair. Tom and Louis were at the bottom of the stairs to meet me. He and Darren chorused that I did indeed look as beautiful as I did when I had my hair. Of course I did, I was the same person who had gone upstairs a few hours earlier. You can look beautiful with or without hair. It's just hair. It can grow again but I had a mission to complete first. People are just used to seeing you with hair but inside you are the same beautiful person. Eventually people do look past it and see you for who you are. They just have to adjust the same as you.

I felt surprisingly OK, a little bit lifted and relieved that the worst was over. I had to remind myself that the hair loss was not forever. But every time I looked in the mirror I was shocked again. Almost like I had forgotten. It was going to be an uphill struggle but it could only get better and I was smiling again. I still wasn't used to the feel of the scarf and spent the rest of the evening constantly tilting my head, touching my head, pulling the scarf back into place. We all sat down to watch TV to get some normality back to our Sunday when we all suddenly became aware of the amount of cancer adverts that were on TV, on every channel. Were these all directed at me? Had they waited for me to give them the bald nod then air them? Images of a girl sitting in a barber's chair having her head shaved! Been there, done that, got it all over my t-shirt, literally. Usually adverts are on for two or three minutes and you only half watch or half listen, yet now they were all around me, pointing at me from the screen. I now understood exactly what they were saying and I would cry whenever they appeared, still feeling isolated. I could truly understand how these brave yet beautiful ladies, and men, who experience alopecia truly feel. Yet stand back, ignore the hair, you are still there. It just allows your beauty to shine through a lot more.

A day or so later I received a letter from my GP to say they were sorry to hear of my diagnosis and that if I needed to go and speak to them at any time, they were there for me. I decided that maybe I needed a little bit of outside help and a chat, so the following morning, after sleeping in a woolly hat to keep my head warm, I made an appointment to see my doctor. I managed to get an appointment a couple of days later by telling the receptionist the reason the doctor wanted to see me.

It was quite therapeutic to relay to the doctor the events that had been going on and he assured me that everything I was doing was right. He also assured me that the survival rate of breast cancer was on the increase and he was still seeing patients who were treated over 20 years ago, and many had no re-occurrence of the disease. This was what I needed to hear. Over the last few months I had spent long enough with doctors, lying on examination beds, having numerous blood tests, always dreading the news that it was terminal, receiving letters and now I was leaving my GP more positive than when I went in.

As I walked through the waiting room it felt like all eyes were on me. People would openly stare, some would look down to their magazines embarrassed that you had eye contact with them. I could hear all their questions, "Why is she wearing a headscarf? What's odd about her appearance?" and some blatantly staring at me trying to take in what they were looking at. I was now the subject of people's conversations, other people's gossip, "Guess who's got cancer?"

I didn't need to wear a t-shirt explaining to them what was wrong, I had the ashen face, the dark rings under my eyes, wrapped up warm because I was continually cold and without hair. All the hallmarks of cancer. I wanted to shout, "Yes, take a good look, I'm wearing a headscarf!" And what were they looking at? Me or cancer? Me with cancer? The look of the overwhelming sadness I felt said it all. I would feel panicked putting family members through the ordeal of walking around with me wearing a headscarf as it just drew attention to us all. I asked my dad one day as we were set to go shopping if it bothered him. "Not at all!" was his reply. But, the fighter in me was still there. My spirit had gone a little in the last few days, but it was soon back.

Cancer, you've taken my hair and part of my body, but that's it, the fight is well and truly back on! I was keeping my baldy head firmly under my hat!

CHAPTER 16 – BALD AND BRAVE

By the third week of my recovery I was feeling OK, and certainly better than I had felt in week one. Because I knew that by the following week after my second session of chemotherapy, I would be back to being knocked off my feet with my bum on the "poorly" chair. I planned to re-stock the freezer, clean the house, do the laundry and get my work up to date. I was getting my bald head round the pending second treatment and I was up for the fight again.

Darren and I arrived at the hospital and took a seat in the waiting room of the Chemotherapy Suite. I saw the oncologist on this day as a few days before I had been for a blood test to check my white blood cell level. This was a procedure before treatment but the results showed that the count was too low and the treatment was postponed. I was stunned. God no! I had mentally prepared myself and I had set milestones of dates to get by. This cancellation would mean that all my plans were delayed. They gave me a week for another blood test and suggested a course of daily GCSF injections to aid the production of my white cells to build me back up for the next treatment. Whilst having to neck a few more tablets too.

"Can you administer the injection yourself?" the oncologist asked.

"Absolutely no way!" was my reply. The reply took no thinking and for me that was the end of that conversation.

He looked at Darren who explained that although he was happy to do it, with my fear of needles he would end up chasing me round the house. When they both glanced at me with a silent look hoping I would change my mind, I looked back at them with the "absolutely not, no way, never" look that I can do quite well. I then explained to the oncologist that I had felt violently sick after the first treatment and it was agreed that after my next he would add some anti-sickness tablets to my ever-growing prescription.

It was arranged for a district nurse to visit daily for five days to give me a booster injection. This wouldn't be administered in my arm, oh no, nothing so simple. It was to be injected into my stomach and would carry on over a five day period, a week after each treatment to ensure there were no more delays.

A different nurse would come every day, and they would admire my home and let slip that their colleague had told them how nice it was from the previous day. I would list the places I had bought things from as they ooh'd and aah'd and distracted me from the snapping sound of the needle in my tummy as it would project the solution via a spring.

My immune system was now at an all-time low so the house was full of anti-bacterial soap and wipes and I had very few visitors. As the doorbell usually only brought the nurse, I didn't make too much of an effort dressing up. One morning was no exception and when the doorbell rang I shuffled to the door with my joggers and sweatshirt on, pale face with yellow rings under my eyes and the usual woolly hat to keep my head warm. I opened the door to be faced by a shocked Jehovah's Witness. We surprised each other. I gasped and she took a step back. I felt like I had answered the door naked. As she backed off apologising I told her I was expecting the nurse. She kindly told me she would add me to her prayers, I obviously looked like I needed all the help I could get, and after she wished me well for a speedy recovery, she was gone. Funny really, someone who you usually dread to see when you open the door, I had managed to get rid of her with no real effort, but she had been terribly kind and unknowingly became yet another person in that ever-growing support network I was creating. Days later, she delivered a handmade card to wish me well. Such a kind thought.

My kitchen was littered with daily and emergency tablets and a bright yellow bucket for used syringes. All that and the fact I was bald, pale, gaining weight due to the steroids and the weird food cravings, coupled with the flu-like symptoms from the daily injections. Each day as I shuffled into the kitchen and looked round at my current life, I felt worse and worse. I never woke up and thought, "Wow, I feel good today!" But I would continue to tell myself that, "Tomorrow I will feel a little bit better."

My food cravings had moved from chicken and chips to cheese crisps then to a particular popular chocolate bar to chocolate eclair cakes. At one point, in my junkie-like state trying to get my fix, I nearly wrote the car off as I sped to the shop. If there weren't a nice big handful of chocolate bars in the kitchen cupboard, Darren and Tom would be faced by a crazed bald woman having withdrawal symptoms. Oddly though, the cravings changed after each treatment. Perhaps I was working my way through the junk food chain!

My mum and Sarah came to visit during the small window of recovery between the chemotherapy treatments as I was feeling slightly better. Since they weren't seeing me on a daily basis, they could see the change in me. I tried to jolly everyone along that I was "doing fine, feeling fine," but really I was finding it harder and harder to put a brave face on it when really I looked ill, and I felt ill. As we all sat down with a cup of tea, I took off my skull-cap and scarf so they could see my head. The hair was patchy and was still coming out, some of it attached to the skull-cap. Both of them sat on the settee and their eyes filled with tears. Sarah couldn't say anything and my mum jumped up, came over and kissed my patchy, yet nicely shaped head. I was used to what it looked like, but they weren't. My mum then tearily said, "I've never seen you without hair." When I was born I had a full head of dark thick hair, so this was new for all us. Sarah still didn't move but a hot tear rolled down her cheek and as she smiled at me through her quivering mouth, it said it all really. We were being terribly brave and not wanting to upset the other when really you wanted to sob really loudly and shout, "It isn't fair!"

I could not look any worse than I did now, hopefully, and practically everyone I knew or cared about had seen me at my lowest. My girlfriends had come round one evening and I had unveiled my patchy, but remember, not coned, beautifully shaped, head. More tears and then one suggested that they should all shave their heads as a sign of sisterly solidarity but I politely insisted that they didn't. Cancer had taken my hair, it was not to take theirs too. I was being bald and brave.

A week later I was back for treatment two after a successful blood test. I was mentally prepared this time to sit with other patients to have the treatment administered by the nurse as I knew what to expect. As it was administered, my adenoids burned from the metallic flavour that drowned my nasal passages and throat as the nurse slowly injected me. People around me were having the intravenous drip for their cancers, some were reading and some were, horror of horrors, eating! Eating was the last thing on my list. I was already feeling the waves of nausea as the cold fluid started to freeze my right arm and my mouth tasted like I had been sucking on a bag of old pennies that had been lying in the back pockets of a very old pair of trousers.

I'd been home for four hours when I hit the wall again. It feels like when you are sitting on a plane and someone opens the overhead compartment. You are just waiting for the smack on the head from a poorly stored bag dropping! But I was prepared. Pyjamas already on, positioned on the "poorly" chair, but the sickness won this time. Although they had promised anti-sickness pills we had been told at the hospital that they weren't on the prescription. The nausea came so quickly that sometimes I couldn't react in time, and at one point found myself on all fours, in the hallway being sick into my pink bucket. All dignity gone as I couldn't even get to the toilet. Darren scraped me off the floor and put me gently back onto the settee. We tried to work out what was best and thought that if I was in bed asleep I wouldn't be sick. Wrong! Thank heavens for the pink bedside bucket which Darren spent the night emptying, all night in fact, and all through the next day.

By 3pm the following day I was being violently sick every ten minutes, and at one point cried out down the toilet "God help me!" which echoed around the bathroom. My body was convulsing, I was retching and I was getting weaker. Darren began to feel helpless and desperate so he rang the specialist nurse in the Chemotherapy Suite. After a few questions, she told him to get me in the car and back to the hospital immediately. I found out later that he'd been told that for me to be so violently sick from chemotherapy could cause my organs to shut down. I didn't think that I could make it to the car but he couldn't let on just how dangerous it was for me not to go. Despite his inner panic he knew he had to keep it together because right at that moment he was the only one who could save me. I was completely reliant on him as he part-carried me down the stairs, my whole body shaking, my feet dragging underneath me whilst clinging to my pink bucket. With a raging temperature I continued to bring up this burning hot yellow metal fluid. I sensed then that if this carried on for much longer the end was a lot closer than I had thought.

He threw my coat round my shoulders and my vomit-stained pyjamas and bundled me into the car. There was no time to look, or smell pretty, we had to get to Leicester Royal Infirmary and fast. We were taken straight through to the Assessment Unit in the Cancer Ward as Darren searched for a familiar cardboard bowl to stick under my chin to aid the sickness as we decided to keep the pink "vomit smelling" bucket in the car. Finally, an oncologist arrived and I part-explained, helped again by Darren, that I had not held fluids in for 24 hours and was continually vomiting metallic bile. As the oncologist was talking, I held up my hand every few minutes to make her pause, always so polite, as I heaved more of it into the cardboard bowl. See? Told you! As I wanted to point to my freshly produced vomit!

An injection of anti-sickness was administered but did not

touch the sides and she demanded fluids, a drip and an elephant sized anti-sickness injection, which was so big it bruised my arm. Suddenly, I was surrounded by a flurry of three nurses administering tubes and fluids. I asked Darren for a drink of lemonade I had been craving after spotting it in the vending machine, just to take some of this metallic taste away. He looked at the oncologist for permission, who said yes. After another bout of sickness I looked at her through tired watery eyes and said, "This was not supposed to happen. You didn't help me." Right at that moment I didn't care how or what she thought, or even how it sounded, no-one could have felt as bad as I did. Because I had told them I "felt" sick, rather than I had "been" sick, the tablet had not been put on my prescription as it was expensive and I was not deemed to be at risk. Well, take a good look at me now. I needed that tablet on my prescription. I needed that tablet in my system and now I was a bigger cost to the NHS.

I was put on a drip and an alarmed monitor, which would go off every time I moved. We learned how to switch it off so a nurse didn't have to keep rushing over and it was agreed I should spend the night on the ward for observation. I was the youngest there. I was bloated, hot from my raging temperature, dehydrated and my kidneys ached as I had not passed my pink pee!

Darren, exhausted, decided I was in the best place and therefore he was able to go home. I put my hot, attractively shaped, head on a cool pillow and drifted off only to be woken every few minutes for a blood pressure check. This would panic me slightly as it could not be taken from my left arm having had some of the lymph nodes removed. I wore a tape bracelet on my hand to indicate this but still panicked when the trolley approached. They had given me a sleeping tablet which was pointless because they also woke me for more tablets, a mouthful of water and the alarm continued throughout the night. Another side effect of the chemotherapy is the feeling of a bruised head. It was so incredibly tender. At least I knew the treatment had reached this area! I had drifted off again, only to be woken this time by the arrival of another patient at 5am. Did she settle down to sleep? No, she decided to call someone on her mobile phone!

"Guess what? They've only put me on the bloody cancer ward."

She was now surrounded by awake cancer patients who had all been trying to get a half decent night's sleep. I could have left it, but funnily enough, I had cancer, and it gave me a lot of symptoms, but one of them wasn't deafness. So in the dark I shouted out, nice and clear, "Some of us DO have cancer on this bloody ward." She was thoughtless, I was exhausted, and she shut up!

After an assessment the next morning I was told that if I ate and kept down some wholemeal toast, I could go home. Even if I had to wire my jaw shut, that toast was staying down because I wanted to go home. I messaged an update to family, as I wasn't up to talking to anyone just yet through my clenched teeth. I sent a text to Darren to come and fetch me and he arrived just as they brought my bin bag of new tablets. Lunch began to arrive and I needed to get out before I was force-fed hospital soup, which I couldn't guarantee would stay down, even on a good day. I wanted to get home, as I also couldn't face being surrounded by gravely ill patients, and after my little outburst with the mobile phone muppet I felt like a fraud taking a bed. See? I still couldn't and didn't want to identify myself as ill as them.

Chemotherapy slows down the body's system so I was now, along with everything else, suffering from constipation and before you say it, I'll say it for you, "Accountants can work it out with a pencil!" Funny! I had fluids to help "aid movement" and the nurses suggested a good walk would get my organs activated. But I was feeling weaker and weaker and recovery was getting slower as the evil juice was being topped up in my body.

One day I was leaning on Darren as we set off for a well planned walk. As we left the front door, down the path, we stopped, turned round and headed back to the house. That was as far as I could manage. All in slow motion, one foot in front of the other, legs feeling like lead, exhausted. I had layers of warm clothing as the lack of blood cells meant I was cold to the touch and could not get warm. Day by day, Darren wrapped me up and made me walk further and further. Each time it felt like a trek and I honestly thought I was never going to be able to walk any distance again. Everything was in slow motion, even my bodily functions!

Family checked in regularly, Sarah called and I told her, in some detail, of things not being passed down below, "I'm trying everything and anything." I had re-visited the Assessment Unit as I was now in some pain but again I was given a course of laxatives and sent home after their concerns that I was not passing anything. Three healthy meals a day had no effect at all, and now after ten days, I was either going to burst or continue walking around like a blimp. Over the counter treatments were having no effect except making me heave and playing havoc with my indigestion. Again, this was not good because chemotherapy has to pass through your bodily waste and this was going nowhere. It was all stuck inside me. Bearing in mind we were nearing Christmas I chomped my way through some nice metallic tasting brussel sprouts with a dessert of metallic tasting Christmas chocolates. And hey presto! Success! My new cure for constipation! Just need to find a cure for cancer now.

Treatment three was Boxing Day. I enviously watched everyone else's Christmas jollity as I felt like I had been hit by a truck, which had then reversed over me and hit me again. I managed to drink, and hold on to, a well-earned sherry. I wasn't parting with that! I would give anything up except my Christmas sherry!

A few days before, my girlfriends and I had a pre-Christmas celebration at one of their houses and I needed to leave early because I was tired. They all lined up by the door to say goodnight and gave me a hug and a kiss. I was hugely flattered and will never forget this simple gesture which meant so much. At this party one of my male friends told me that they had discussed that out of the ten girls present, if they had to pick one who would cope with a cancer diagnosis it would be me. Now, there's a compliment in there somewhere, because as far as they were concerned I had the strength and determination to cope with it. This was based on watching me raise my son alone, and get through all the things that life had thrown at me. But cancer?

Boxing Day, and no Christmas leftovers for me, but back to the Chemotherapy Suite, which was heaving with patients. Even cancer doesn't take Christmas off. I gave the staff a tin of my new found laxative Christmas chocolates to maintain the Christmas spirit. Getting the line into the back of my hand was difficult on this one, as the vein had collapsed. They tried everything, wrapping me up in blankets like a big Christmas parcel, putting my hands in warm water and lowering my hands in the hope that gravity would work. After a series of attempted stabs we found one that would take the treatment but still risked the leak into the tissue. So, another battle in this war, my veins were showing signs of giving up.

More and more sessions of this procedure takes its toll, the symptoms get worse and last longer. It takes more and more out of you and you do not recover as quickly as you did the last time. Is this what death feels like? Slowly creeping up on you? During my recovery period I would make a point of lying on the settee with my back to the stairs so that Tom would not be able to see me. He would quietly come down, say nothing but rest his warm hand on my shoulder, and I could feel his love and support. He was being so strong in dealing with all of this and it meant the world to me. Nothing had to be said. For the moment I couldn't actively protect him, but I was doing everything I could to stay around. I was determined for his sake that I was not going anywhere. I was, and always will be his mum.

It was January 2012 and being at home a lot and a cat lover, I scrolled through the cat rescue centres, like one does when they are bored, looking for an unwanted cat that could be a buddy for Louis and another companion for me. There she was! It was a freezing Sunday and like always I was donning my woolly hat. I did not want to be refused an animal at the rescue centre in case they thought I was not going to be around for long. I was coated in make up so Darren and I headed out on our mission. We found her, we loved her and we named her Clawdia. The instant we returned home she took over! Louis didn't know what had hit him. I think the supermarket lorry had less clout. We didn't know what had hit us! She was full of character and the softest fur I had ever felt. She took full control of the household like a female does and she helped me massively with my recovery. I was too occupied with the two cats to think of my illness!

I had three remaining chemotherapy treatments with the same procedures. Arrive at the suite's waiting room, treatment administered, forgetting the mints to disguise the metallic taste and experiencing the strange cravings on my return home. I craved chicken and chips, cakes, cheese and onion sandwiches and still cheese crisps! I had no clue why! Quickly enough, I was taking my last treatment and had finally remembered the mints. This was the hardest session and I was determined that when it was done, that was it, I would never put myself through this again. It had become almost impossible to remember that chemotherapy was your friend, not your enemy. It is fighting the real enemy as much as you are, although at the time it does not feel like it. I thought of it as an internal jet wash, rushing through my veins, killing every blood cell in its path. I was often amazed that it didn't just burn through everything like a forest fire and kill every organ and tissue in its way. It is amazing how it works and it truly is your valued friend!

I had the final treatment of chemotherapy on February 27th 2012. Sarah's birthday!

By now, my hair had gone completely. And I mean everywhere! My eyebrows looked like a child had attacked them with a pair of scissors, my eyelashes snapped off to the touch, my nails were ridged and brittle. I didn't look like me any more, all my features had faded to almost nothing. People would stare, particularly when I was out, doing a second look to work out what was wrong, different, odd, looking to see if they recognised me. Others would stare, unashamedly horrified, as if you should never had left the house. I should have walked around with a bell calling out "unclean, unclean." The only place I felt "normal" these days was at the hospital, where it was expected. It was like a second home and it was somewhere I could relax. People came to see me at home, those who knew and cared for me, my family, Darren's family, my friends. But they could never disguise that slight look of initial shock when they first saw me no matter how normal they tried to behave. I felt and looked like death, but would immediately become the jovial, perky Clare Bear, as much to cheer myself as to put them at ease so they wouldn't be afraid to re-visit. Darren's grandmother had offered to buy me an expensive wig, which was a lovely gesture, but I refused as I assured her that the hair loss was temporary. I didn't want her to waste her money in a kindly attempt to make me feel pretty, and I was coping with wearing the headscarves even though they would turn on my head and be wonky by the end of the day so I would resort to the woolly hat. Everyone was trying to do something to feel helpful, anything to help me get through it, but really there was nothing, just time. We all had to wait and be patient.

Before my last treatment I had booked a morning appointment held at the hospital with "Look Good, Feel Better" for advice on make-up and hair-loss, which is really a lesson in re-building your confidence. I can't say I was particularly looking forward to it as I would have to expose my baldness to a whole new set of people. Thankfully, because it was still winter, walking around in a big woolly hat didn't attract many stares and I could be free in the anonymity of a crowd situation in the shops. Not everyone judged you, but if you took on an anonymous role, the second you stepped out with a pretty scarf on your head, trying to make an effort but exposing your "cancer" to everyone, I discovered that individuals made you feel freakish.

There was always the exception though, and one day Darren had taken me out for the day to Derbyshire. I will never forget one lady who passed me and we had made eye contact for a couple of seconds. She could see my fear and she looked directly at me, smiled and winked. Things like that would boost my confidence immeasurably, knowing that someone else understood and the reassurance that I was "OK." She made my day, and I added her to my ever-growing list of supporters. Simple gestures like that, the acknowledgement that you're not alone, builds the ability to carry on in your bid to be normal. It's a lesson in humanity, and today, with my full head of hair, I too smile at ladies wearing headscarves. I know their fear and I know what courage it takes to leave the comfort of your home. I know what they are feeling, I know what it feels like to be isolated, as if you're the only one in the world feeling like this. I know how it feels to be that scared because you have still not been given the all-clear, and I now know how much better a simple gesture of eye contact with a smile can make you feel. So at your most fearful time hoping that you will survive, the world is not there to support you. Just the ones who understand.

As it turned out, the make-up session was fabulous with the volunteer beauticians and other patients. I was given a bag of goodies, which matched my skin type, and the room was full of cackling, chatting, biscuit chomping, mainly bald and now confident women. We were free to discuss our chemotherapy, our operations, and the pending treatments, an immediate bond, which boosted me just a little bit more. There were compliments bouncing all around the room as we were transformed from featureless women, to bald but beautiful women. We had restored our identities. I enjoyed myself for the first time in months, and met some lovely people. By the end of the session I was to keep the goody bag of make-up, perfume and a fully made up face, which I was now sure I would be able to recreate. But I did. For the first time in months I started to look like me again, and rather than the gaunt cancer victim I would be able to go shopping and be "accepted" again. As a treat, and a bit of a test, I stopped at the retail park on my way home and shopped for THREE HOURS. I was confident and was smiling on the inside as well as on the outside. I felt like me again. I had been given some freedom. Darren rang to ask where I was. "Are you coming home yet?"

"Nope!" I replied. That was all he needed to hear as yet again I was being bald and brave.

CHAPTER 17 – WITH OR WITHOUT YOU

I convinced myself that I needed to go into "cat recovery mode" and to sleep to aid my recovery. If I shut myself down, maybe the chemotherapy would work more effectively. As I lay on the settee, my breathing would rattle as the liquid gathered in the back of my nose and throat. Sometimes, if I was completely motionless and frozen to the touch, Darren would come over to check if I was still breathing. This could not have been easy and I was not always aware he was doing it. Sometimes, the snorting and gargling noise would wake me up, from what sounded like the death rattle.

One night he came in from work, and saw me lying motionless

on the sofa. He walked quietly across the room and knelt down next to me. This night I was so low, so ill and so weak, I really thought this might be it and I might not make it through. Even my breathing felt laboured. I slowly moved my eyes to fix on his and as we looked at each other, one single tear rolled effortlessly down my cheek and I quietly told him I didn't think I could fight this any longer. I had no strength and just the simple movement of sitting up and making it to the toilet had become a momentous task. I was exhausted. His warm hand reached out and held my limp cold one, and he quietly, but firmly said with tears in his eyes that I had to fight as I had everything to live for. I knew what he was saying was right but I had forgotten what it felt like to feel well. I was convinced I would never feel well again but I had to keep fighting with the tiny bit of strength I had left.

Tomorrow I will feel a little bit better.

Sleeping in my woolly hat had become a must. I would wake in the night and discover it had come off and I would search the bed for it. I was usually lying on it so it was always nice and warm when I pulled it back onto my head. Sometimes the hat would be twisted across my face as I slept so I would turn in the night and the hat would stay where it was! You don't appreciate how much your hair protects you and keeps you warm and now my head ached with the cold, feeling constantly bruised from the chemotherapy.

One morning I woke and took my woolly hat off. Darren must have thought he was sleeping with a builder! Lying on my side looking at him, I wanted some reassurance that I was beautiful, so I asked him.

"Do I look like Demi Moore?"

He studied me for a second, then replied, "You look more like Roger Moore!"

We laughed and laughed and laughed. It helped. Bizarrely.

Along with the list of symptoms that seemed to be growing daily from chemotherapy, I was suffering from memory lapses, a symptom known as "Chemo Brain," (or "Chemo-Brian" if you have predictive text on your phone and you're trying to explain it to someone!) Anyway, I would use words in the wrong places (usually swear words) or completely forget the word I need to use. I would get really frustrated which led to me getting angry. One evening I was trying to explain something to Darren and needed to use the word "table." My mind was a complete blank. The word had gone and I couldn't finish what I was trying to say to him. Finally, I had to point at it until he said the word for me. It was like some ridiculous game of charades and I thought I was going slightly mad until I discovered it is a recognised symptom.

So, moving into February 2012, I was still on this rollercoaster ride of feeling ill, feeling better, discovering another symptom, having to deal with real life while still battling this silent, deadly squatter inside me. It never ceased to surprise me. Just when I thought that maybe, by now, I was nearing the end of the ride and I could get off, it had another surprise in store. I had been called back for my repeat cervical smear test and I was convinced that after all of the chemotherapy, there was no way I could have a cancerous cell in my body. So, the new confident me, strode in for her appointment, only to have the results back, "Abnormal Cells Present/Borderline." What kind of hellish practical joke was this? How the heck could that happen? After all this, it hadn't gone? I was back down at my lowest point again and I was scared. The treatment hadn't killed the cancer and now it was killing me. I would have to wait a further six months as it was suggested that it may just be an abnormal reading because of all the treatment. But six months is a long time to wait for confirmation and now I was really worried that I may not live long enough to find out.

I needed time to be alone to think, so I ran a big bubble bath. I slipped down into the warm water with just my bald head above the surface and I stared for a long time at the bubbles which looked like clouds. I was almost in a trance and shut everything out around me, just staring at the bubbles. Then I imagined myself above the clouds, looking down at Tom and then sobbed and sobbed. The usual hot tears, running down my face into the soapy water. I sobbed for my sorry pitiful state, the state I looked and I sobbed for Tom. He was being so strong and supportive and keeping life "normal" for me. I could not let this happen, I could not give in, I was not ready to go and I had to claw back some of the control. I was fighting each battle and winning, but it felt like I was losing the war. But I couldn't, I wouldn't let all this negativity eat me up, so I pushed myself up and out of the water, left all the negative thoughts in the bath, dried myself, slipped into my warm "special" pyjamas and sat with my positive thoughts and my baldy head next to him on the sofa. I was planning on staying around a little bit longer, and right now, nothing and no-one was taking that away from me.

In all this, there were some times that I felt as close to death as I ever imagined to be. Mostly when I was completely immobile, I seriously felt that if the worst was to come, I had to be practical. Being my usual organised self, I started to plan my own funeral. It may sound a bit ghoulish now, but at the time, it was almost like a sense of calm and I knew I had to be sensible. This was real life after all. Did I honestly want to leave this task to everyone I was leaving behind? What kind of conversations would they have – "What was her favourite piece of music?", "Is there a reading she particularly liked?" There was no reason anyone would necessarily know the answers to these questions, as we had never needed to have the conversation before. Why would I want to put anyone I cared about through making these decisions? Had I not put them through enough already?

So, with all these questions I put together my last wishes. If I did not make it through, I wanted to know that I had given Tom the best future possible I could in my absence. I had done what I could to this point, but he was still only 16, and I would have to reluctantly pass the baton on to someone else. I requested that the cats would stay with him if possible, and the house would either be sold or rented and the money invested wisely to secure his future. I was happy for him to take personal possessions from the home, but he was not to stay there alone with the memories. I didn't want him to walk through the door hoping and praying that I would be sitting there waiting for him or that I would be coming home at some point. It breaks my heart now just thinking of it.

These are not decisions I ever thought I would have to make at age 42. I had chosen the music that meant something to me. I was to arrive at the church with a lone bagpiper walking ahead of the hearse playing *Amazing Grace,* then into the church with *Ave Maria* and my Catholic upbringing ensured that I remembered the words in Latin to this day. If he felt able, I would have liked Tom to say something, maybe something about me, but as a way of thanking all the people who were there for me, and for him. I hoped it would give him strength, but maybe it would just all be too much, for everyone. He would also benefit from seeing the people there supporting him and it would be something he could take with him into the future, knowing that the support was always there. I chose a special song from me to him, which was to be The Mamas & the Papas *Dedicated To The One I Love.* I felt the words were very fitting and they were words I didn't need to say as they were all there written beautifully in the song. Another one of my favourites, U2's *With Or Without You* which I thought would be nice during the ceremony, and finally, when I was leaving the church, Linkin' Park's *Shadow of the Day*. I wanted to be interred at my favourite time of the day, sunset, which I am guessing is impossible. The lyrics I'm referring to? "And the sun will set for you."

These plans were very personal to me, you understand, no-one knew of any of these arrangements. I didn't want to hear "Don't be silly, you'll get through this," because let's face it, no-one really knew. I wanted a private meeting with the Father at my local Catholic Church, as although my will would have all the necessary practical details, I wanted to tell him my most private wishes that could be shared with others when he was administering the last rites. My mourners were to wear pink and donate to a cancer hospice. I had even worked out the menu for my wake. Nothing too complicated or extravagant:

Chicken and chips

Cheese flavoured crisps

Chocolate bars

Chocolate éclair cakes

Cheese and onion sandwiches

And if you recognise any of these gourmet delights, it means you have been reading my previous chapters, because these, my dear reader, are all the things I had craved during chemotherapy which all weirdly begin with a "C!" If I had managed to eat it, then the people at my service could share in my wide and varied menu without a vegetable in sight!

Anyway, there might have been a celebrity feel to the whole event, if Peter Andre turned up. Why Peter Andre? Oh, haven't I mentioned him before? Chemo Brain again. I told you I was having trouble with my memory. Years ago, an ex-boyfriend was working in the same building where Peter Andre attended a gym. One Sunday morning, I was fed up as he had been working away all week including the weekend and when he called me he said, "I have someone here who wants to talk to you." After a slight pause, I heard an Australian accent, and thought it was one of his colleagues messing about. He'd spoken to Peter in the week and had told me how polite he had been.

After I'd initially told him I didn't quite believe it was him, he continued in his very polite way to convince me otherwise. It was too good to be true, but it really was him as there was no ridiculous laddish banter. He said, "I understand you cook a mean Sunday roast?" By now, I was fully convinced it was him, and I became all ridiculous and giggly (for goodness sake woman, pull yourself together! This is only an attractive celebrity who happens to be chatting to you on a Sunday morning whilst you are wearing your pyjamas and bed hair!) He had asked me if he was in the area could he pop in for dinner! So, Peter Andre wanted to come to my house for my Sunday roast? That's something to tell the grandchildren! We ended on a cheery note, and for all you doubters out there, he then sent me a kind note as confirmation of his need for my roast dinner! Sadly, over the years, after countless house-moves, I lost the note. Sorry Peter but you are still welcome for dinner.

That little tale was to lighten the mood a bit, as I don't want you to think I spent all these months being maudlin and thinking about death. My real aim was that I wanted to be remembered for the healthy, life-loving person I was, not the poor cancer sufferer who had been taken too soon. I wanted flowers. I always want flowers, who doesn't? I keep them in the house constantly to honour the child I miscarried many years ago. For me, the growth, the blossoming and the beauty of flowers replaces loss of the physical presence of a child and gives me something that brings an acceptance of what wasn't meant to be. It's all I have as there is no grave or place to mourn.

So, finally, once you've all wept inconsolably through my service, at the very bottom of my service sheet would be one last piece of advice that I could share – Check Your Breasts! Check Your Parts! And that goes for every single person out there, men and women alike! It's the simplest of things, something that could alter your life course for the better. Then, dearest friends, I could rest in peace, with or without you!

CHAPTER 18 – HERO IN SCRUBS

In the hope that I would not need to discuss my funeral arrangements any further, the chemotherapy ended on 27th February 2012. This was followed by more attentive check ups because I had already been told that the next step was further surgery to get rid of the squatter, hopefully for good. These decisions are not made by one person as your whole case is presented to a board called the "MDT" or Multidisciplinary Team. This is a team of highly qualified professionals, made up of oncologists, surgeons, breast care nurses and so on, who use their knowledge and expertise to decide the stages of your treatment. So, donning an attractive headscarf and my newly found make up techniques, Darren and I returned to the Glenfield Breast Care Centre, so we could find out what was to happen next. It was now March 2012, and I was due to meet my new surgeon. I was really worried as he didn't know me, I didn't know him and he hadn't operated on me before. Was he familiar enough with my case and did he know what he was doing?

We checked in at the reception and Darren and I walked into the examining room where I was asked to remove my top half of clothes and put on the infamous three-ribboned gown, or attempt to, at least! As I fidgeted, my new surgeon appeared from the side door with a breast care nurse. Wow! He was not what I was expecting! He was as old as me! Was he qualified? How long has he been doing this job? Can I see your CV? (Just to reassure you, I Googled him when I got home, as you do, and discovered that he truly knows his stuff. He is internationally acclaimed and highly respected in his field. This man knows his boobs! If you know what I mean?)

He waded through my records, my previous operation and my chemotherapy treatment and we talked for ages. He was in no rush, I had a life-threatening disease and he wanted to make sure we were both on the same page in terms of my treatment. He mentioned the recently retired surgeon who still asked about me, who said he was frustrated that he hadn't managed to "finish the job!" I think I knew what he meant! But with this new surgeon, I felt an instant bond of trust and felt secure putting my life in his hands. He explained the upcoming operation in detail. I was having a left breast re-excision of supero-medial margin and rotational lateral flap for breast re-shaping. Between you and me, this means that they needed to remove tissue from the upper area of the breast to ensure a clear margin, but the chances of my breast collapsing onto my chest wall were high. So, once he'd removed the tissue, he would make a 180 degree cut, peel back the skin (hope you're not eating), twist up the tissue to replace what he had removed with my own breast tissue and sew me back together again. He explained that as I had youth on my side, I had ample breast tissue to make the reconstruction easier and retain my "full" breasts. Well, there's a few adjectives every woman wants to hear! When he said that he might have to remove my nipple and sew it back on, the back of my knees went a bit funny.

I then had to prepare myself for a course of radiotherapy to assist my recovery. He asked if he could take photos of my breasts because he wanted to show future patients the effect of post-lumpectomy and then the effect and recovery of the rotation flap procedure when it went ahead. I asked when they would appear on social media to which he politely replied that they were solely for his records! Aside from all the medical jargon, I really felt this man cared and his confidence rubbed off on me. Wednesday 11th April 2012 was put in the diary for my pre-assessment for surgery. Then another date was set, Friday 20th April 2012 for the second surgery. So, in nine days' time, my un-invited squatter would be completely evicted.

The day quickly arrived and I used my sterile wash, which made my skin tighter than tight. I hadn't experienced that feeling for a long time, so forget Botox and face lifts, give this stuff a bash! The decision was made to leave Tom at home this time. Darren and I arrived at Glenfield Hospital and I was shown to my allocated bed so I could unpack and get settled. I was now a dab hand at these procedures and no sooner had I opened my holdall than the anaesthetist arrived and asked me to put on a gown. Yes, that infamous gown again! I was to be the first patient in surgery! No time to think! Do I need a nervous wee? My body isn't answering. DO I NEED A NERVOUS WEE? Heck, just go and try.

Darren and I struck up conversation with two elderly ladies in the beds opposite, both of whom had undergone double mastectomies the day before and they had nothing but praise and admiration for their surgeons and the care they were receiving. They were both in their nineties and looked fabulous. Well done girls! There's a lesson for us all!

Nurses were in and out, blood pressure taken, checking name, date of birth, checking, checking and checking. This reminded me of a day I had taken my old cat, Spot, to the vet. The receptionist asked, "What's the name?" and I said "Spot." She then said, "And the animal's name?" Huh? I started to laugh and said, "Sorry, no, my name's not Spot!" She wasn't fazed at all and had no idea as to what I had found amusing.

The surgeon and his assistant arrived and led me to a side room. They wanted to draw around my breast as a guide to know exactly where to cut. He had a blue marker pen and asked me to sit on the side of the bed. After he'd done it, I had to hold out my arm so they could both stand back and admire his artwork, having a quick chat together, then adding a bit more to the line. The comical moment was suddenly lost to me, and I said, "Look, I am 42 years old. If you have to cut my left arm off or need to cut the breast off just do it. I just want to get rid of the cancer." He stepped forward, looked me in the eyes and said firmly, "That will not be necessary." He was happy and confident with his drawing, shook my hand and walked me back to my bed in his true gentleman style. Almost immediately I was being wheeled out to surgery and I called over to one of the ladies I had been chatting to earlier, who had a birthday that day, "Save me some cake!" It was 8.30am and I was determined to be back for lunch and cake!

In the pre-op room we discovered that the anaesthetist had

gone missing! Nothing too dramatic, as she was on a "much-needed" coffee run apparently, but hey guys, I had somewhere I needed to be! A nurse rested her bottom on the side of my trolley bed and started to chat to Darren and me. There had been so much going on, I hadn't had time to think, but now I did. This was reality again and this pause in proceedings caused a huge wave of panic to come crashing over me again. I started asking questions out loud, what if I don't come out of this? Are these my last moments on earth? Then I asked Darren why we had wasted all this time, why we never had any future plans and why we had not got married or at least living together. I didn't have time for an answer because the coffee break was suddenly over and they were waiting for me in the next room. I said goodbye to Darren as I was wheeled through and then I saw my surgeon in his blue scrubs. My Hero in Scrubs! He mouthed, "Are you OK?" A simple question, but at that moment it was everything to me, because I really wasn't OK from the conversation I had just been having and I was terrified, but I smiled the biggest smile I could muster and said, "Yes, thank you." His casual ask of the question made me realise that there was nothing to be worried about. Was he trembling or looking sweaty and nervous when he asked? No. I was in the anaesthetic bay and was able to see through the open double doors of the operating theatre. It was just like you see on TV, big overhead lights, wheeled trays of shiny things, everything white, clean and lots of staff. Lots of them, all chatting about last night's TV or what was on the canteen menu. It was a normal day's work for them. Maybe someone noticed my wide terrified eyes, because someone nudged the doors shut.

The anaesthetist, with her coffee breath, and her assistant then set about trying to find a vein in my right (chemotherapy vein killed) arm and there was nothing. No reaction at all, even with

---

my arm hanging down to the floor, my vein wasn't rising. The assistant slapped the inside of my elbow and the back of my hand and still nothing. It's gone matey, chemo's had it! The continuous slapping was starting to hurt now and I was wondering when it was going to be my turn to start slapping back. We had already wasted half an hour since I had left the ward. I had been on time and I didn't need them to start rushing because of their timetable. Where was Mr Mallet this time? They couldn't use my left arm as this had undergone the removal of lymph nodes, but guess what, the veins were standing upright and dark blue in that arm! They tried everything they could think of, even warm water, dropping my arm, lifting my arm, wrapping it up to warm it and still nothing. I was sore and getting worried and really wanted to say, "Look, thanks for everything, I've had a lovely time, but I'm off."

I knew I wouldn't be able to leave that room conscious and I was getting so cross at the anaesthetist's assistant that he might not be leaving there conscious either. Finally, the anaesthetist decided that the only place that might work would be my right foot! I didn't know they could do that, but I can honestly say that inserting that needle was absolute torture. The assistant needed to hold my foot still for the drug to be administered but my instinct was to keep pulling it up towards me. I was crawling up the bed, half sitting, and half clinging to his arm. I was really hoping I was hurting him after all the slapping, and he kept telling me to lie back and relax while they constantly re-adjusted everything because of my squirming. Relax? Oh the irony! I am hanging on for dear life buddy and onto your arm! For the first time since we'd "met" he looked over his shoulder at my face and told me to lie back, breathe deeply and I would be OK. I don't know which one of us was in more pain and that small window into him treating me like a human being made me do just that and I looked at the clock on the wall. Gosh, would you look at that, it's 10am…then nothing. I was out cold.

Next thing I knew I was staring at the ceiling of the recovery room and someone had slipped my glasses on again. That split second when you wake up trying to work out where you are is not usually followed by the searing pain I suddenly felt through my breast and across my chest. Oh dear Lord, help me! I glanced to one side and saw a recovery nurse sitting by my bed and then I realised that I was still on oxygen with small tubes running up my nose. I had another drip at the back of my hand and the nurse was administering morphine through a machine he was controlling, and not as quickly as I'd had liked, but this seemed more serious recovery than last time.

He asked, "On a scale of one to ten, what would you rate your pain?"

"Ten."

A minute later, "On a scale of one to ten, what would you rate your pain?"

"Ten."

This went on for quite a while until I stabilised but I had to stay connected to oxygen and the morphine drip. It was 2.30pm when I was able to return to the ward, along with my oxygen and morphine. When I arrived, Darren was waiting by the bed and I had missed both lunch and the birthday cake! The curtains were pulled round my bed and the nurses tried to make me more stable by giving me tablets with sips of water. I glanced at my chest to see that not only had I started the day with someone drawing on me with marker pen, but now someone had now lavishly painted me iodine yellow. I could barely move a muscle and I didn't give two hoots, or any hoots for that matter, to wear my get well pyjamas. My hand was now sporting nice big purple bruises, not only from the battering it had received prior to surgery, but also because apparently they had tried to remove the catheter from my foot during surgery and had tried to get it into my wrist or in between my knuckles. Let's just say, pretty much every inch of me hurt.

I was drifting in and out of consciousness when I heard the voice of my surgeon on the other side of the curtain. Darren moved to the end of the bed so the surgeon could stand closer to me and he took my left (un-bruised) hand, "It all went perfectly well," he said. I squeezed his hand back as tightly as I could as I was feeling slightly numb down my left hand side. Tears rolled down my cheeks and I, for once, was speechless. Off my face but speechless. He explained that they did not need to remove and sew my nipple back on and everything else appeared to be successful. Darren joined me in the sobbing. Tonight, this top surgeon would go home to his wife and children and chat about nothing in particular over supper, having no conception of the gratitude I felt towards him at this moment, and what an impact he had on my life. Was I finally going to be saved?

My results would be announced in ten days, and although I didn't want to wait that long before I saw my Hero in Scrubs again, I needed the time to recover. As he made to leave, I held onto his hand a little bit longer wanting him to tell me over and over that I was going to be OK. I started to blub my thank yous through snot bubbles, (not quite like you see on the movies) and wanted him to stay forever telling me I would be OK. He smiled, his fabulous, reassuring, heroic smile, and I finally let go of his hand after giving it one last ridiculously limp squeeze.

Darren shook his hand, a bit more manly I hope, and we finally let him go. He had given me my life back. He was confident and I had more chance of surviving this than I had since the start of it all. I had to remain confident and positive, just like him. This recovery was going to be a harder slog than previously. I was now bruised and battered after two surgeries and months of aggressive chemotherapy which had only ended seven weeks earlier.

I was wearing a "Redivac" drain again with the tube stitched into the left side of my breast, but I was now an old hand at dealing with this. Been there, done that! Hidden it under my t-shirt! The trickiest thing was always going to the bathroom and not catching the stitches. Then I realised I was hungry, really hungry. No lunch, no cake, and I had been "nil by mouth" since 8pm the night before. The nurse found a toffee yogurt and a banana. Hmm, tasty! I started to eat in slow motion, relishing the cold and refreshing feeling on my tongue, but of course I was still being pumped full of morphine which kept making me nod off. This resulted in me suddenly waking up with a snort with a load of warm mashed banana in my mouth. Darren politely read his book in the armchair at my side, probably not wanting to spend too long watching this yellow bald snorting thing in the bed, resembling Homer Simpson, but suddenly he had to spring into action to get a cardboard bowl for all the mashed banana and yogurt that had decided it was not going to stay around for long. You would have thought he would have kept one with him at all times now for these emergencies. I had to remain hungry, semi-conscious and snorty, while Darren went off to ring family who were waiting to find out how I was. After lots of love and good wishes from them all, Darren decided to go home and get some much needed sleep and leave me to drift off into drug crazy dreamland.

After a disturbed night of blood pressure and drip-checks, I had some breakfast, which stayed where it was, and I was then helped to the toilet, my bare bottom on view to the ward because my paper pants had decided to alter their course, still wearing my iodine-stained gown. I was bald, yellow, bruised and sore, but to me I looked gorgeous and I didn't care.

A nurse suggested a wash down in the bathroom, probably after seeing the wreck of me shuffling down the corridor, and it sounded wonderful. It took forever to get to the bathroom, and she made me lean on the sink while she washed my back with a warm soapy flannel. It felt divine, but then I saw stars, and spots, and I started to cold sweat, I was going to keel. She dashed off to get a wheelchair and I had to sit forward with my head as close to my knees as we dared. I hung on to the handrail on the wall, and breathed deeply, desperately trying to get some of the blood back up to my head to keep me upright. Three nurses had to help me back onto the bed, yes three, I was in pain, I was semi-conscious and I had tubes sticking out of me and a partly washed back.

I was then told that the ward was closing that day, and they were sending remaining patients home or to other wards in the hospital. As I was still so weak, and still really not with it, they wanted to put me on the cardiac ward as they had space, but I didn't want to stay longer than I really had to and wanted to go home. Just at that Darren arrived and joined in the discussion.

"Bear, you need to stay in."

"I want to go home. I am going home!"

We found my joggers and zip-up top in my little side cupboard but then realised that I had to try and get into my post-surgery bra to support everything. This is essential and keeps everything tightly packed into place to aid and support surgery rather than everything hanging freely and causing more pain. It had been bought especially for this moment and now the thought of struggling into it was a potential nightmare. I was so swollen (they don't allow for that in the purchase, do they?) that it wouldn't even reach round my back. Hang on, did I care? No, I did not, so I shoved it back in my overnight bag, zipped myself into my top, threw the drain in the floral bag over my shoulder, slowly sank into the wheelchair, waved my goodbyes and I left.

A few days later, the drain was to be removed. I didn't need to watch it this time, snip snip with the stitches, the feeling of unravelling tangled wool again, a piece of clear tape over the wound and it was done. More "thank yous" to the staff and I now only had a few more days to wait for the results of the operation. I was more positive now than I had been for a long time. Surely I can only get better.

And who would be giving me the results? Why, my Hero in Scrubs, of course!

CHAPTER 19 – THE FINAL EVICTION

A few weeks before my last operation I had a visit from one of my clients. He handed me a white box and told me to open it. I was thrilled and tore at the tape and looked inside as he said, "It's for you." Inside were small trays of cakes which we shipped out from the warehouse. OK, momentary disappointment, then confusion. Why would I want a case of these? Politely I said, "Lovely, thank you." He laughed and said, "No, no, take a tray out and read the side of the packaging."

It was a cranberry cake (cranberry to represent pink) with a donation-on-purchase made to Breast Cancer Campaign. I was astounded. Our customer had made a pledge to raise a minimum of £25,000 with a further £12,000 to be donated to the cause. These were being released imminently to major supermarkets and delicatessens and they were doing it in my honour. I logged on to their website and my name appeared. I couldn't believe it, it seems I meant so much to people and had touched their lives in some way. That ever-growing support network became slightly larger. To launch the promotion they had decided to drive the cakes around London in a vintage car and take donations en-route. It was also decided, as part of the campaign, to do a charity bike ride across the South Downs to the South Coast on the 14th April 2012. Some of the guys from work said they would do it and Tom even volunteered. There was no time to waste and we had to get sponsorship, t-shirts and accommodation sorted.

No sooner had we checked bicycle tyre pressures, ensured they were road-worthy and purchased the necessary gel seats, we were off. We popped the bikes onto a carrier who delivered them down south to the start of the route. I was still recovering from the after effects of the chemotherapy and a week after my second surgery, I popped on a pretty headscarf and drove the three volunteer cyclists south. I'm not sure what the reception staff made of the four of us as we arrived to check-in to the hotel, two guys in their twenties, Tom and me, but we dropped our bags in the rooms and headed out to find something to eat.

Any concerns I had for the guys wanting to be seen with me immediately dissolved as I realised they were my friends. Other people stared, something I was acutely aware of, but after supper, we went back to the hotel and headed to our beds to get a good night's sleep to prepare for the early start. It was to be a 40 mile cycle ride so while they sorted out their bikes, their outfits and took photograph's, I climbed into the Land Rover "support vehicle" to follow them. Throughout the journey we stopped at break sites, which also became an opportunity to sell more cakes and raise more money. We had a fabulous day and it was a fabulous turnout. Despite feeling absolutely exhausted, but riding high on adrenalin, I drove home later that night with three sleeping, lightly sore bottomed boys, back to the Midlands. The day had been a success.

I took the opportunity of my hospital visits, for blood tests, pre-assessments and appointments with oncology, to hand out some of the promotional cakes to the members of staff who receive little praise or little acknowledgement. This had never happened before and they were all amazed. They would say things like, "They must think so much of you" and I would think that, yes, do you know, I think they do. And I liked it! I smiled like a Cheshire cat for weeks. For the first time in this difficult journey I felt I was finally winning and I was feeling positive. I had so many people supporting me.

The phlebotomists were thrilled to receive cakes, they were taken to my Hero in Scrubs, my oncologist, the Chemotherapy Suite, my GP surgery, Breast Care Centre, Headstrong, Coping with Cancer, Macmillan Cancer Support and some were saved for the radiotherapy team who I would get to know in the next few weeks. For me and my family, it was thrilling and flattering to think that finally from a very dark place there was a glimmer of light, and don't forget, I still hadn't received my results.

So, the ten days after my surgery came around and Darren and I were back in the Breast Care Centre for my appointment with my Hero in Scrubs. And what was it to be? Good news? Or the dreaded news I didn't want to hear? In the waiting room, cold sweat all over, hands shaking, staring at the floor, constantly replaying in mind the scenarios of what might happen. By now, it was May 2012 and I had nothing but bad news after bad since the previous September. Surely I deserved a break?

Name called, into a side room, top half of my clothes off, the three-ribboned gown, which I recently fashioned into a casual wraparound as I was sick and tired of not being able to do up the ribbons which were placed so that only a contortionist could manage them. We sat quietly and could hear the muffled voices of my Hero and the breast care nurse from the room next door. As they came in, Darren and I sat staring, wide eyed as they sat down. My Hero was smiling, but was it a "good news smile" or was it "I'll put you at your ease smile while I break the bad news?" Desperately trying to read his face, I glanced towards the nurse to see if I could read anything in hers for what was to come. They sat side on to the examining couch, my Hero was holding my very large folder of notes as he looked at me and said, "We were successful!"

Nothing registered. I just sat staring at him not saying anything and not moving. Obviously receiving good news was not what I was used to and it didn't sink in, "We've got it all," my Hero said, then he smiled the biggest smile.

Darren was holding my chemo hand and squeezed all the remaining life out of it, what was left. I still sat there. Motionless. Speechless. Exhausted and numb. After all this, after all our hard work, after all the days and nights staring at the ceiling not sure if I'd ever get through it, was it really all over? Without realising it I was crying and so was Darren. The nurse started to pass me the crap hospital tissues that soak up nothing, as my face was wet with snot and tears. Don't be shocked, I've painted worse pictures for you. This was truly a day I never thought would really happen. I had absolutely prepared myself for the worst. It wasn't the scene from a Hollywood movies with the music starting up in the background, but this was my movie, and this was my happy ending. And I was soaking up every last minute of it (not with the crap hospital tissues because they soak up nothing!) Everyone involved had done what they promised to do all those months ago, I was in their care and they had saved my life.

I squeezed out an insufficient weak "thank you" but it just did not cover it. How could I ever say thank you enough? I could now use the term "cancer survivor" rather than "cancer sufferer." I would have this title for the next five years, then after more assessments I would move even further away from the shadow of cancer sufferer and stay in the next category for another ten years. The black veil that I had been staring through for the last few months was finally being lifted. I could see my future. I would see my son grow. I had been given back my life. My Hero then started to explain what had occurred during surgery, and that tests on the tissue he had removed showed a clear margin, along with the surrounding tissue which also showed clear.

Although my first operation, by my Angel in Scrubs, was successful, my Hero in Scrubs had ensured that they were absolutely certain they had got everything. But my journey was not over. I still had to undergo radiotherapy. Bizarrely, I was fine with the decision. I would still do anything now, anything they told me to do. He examined me thoroughly, checked my wound, and took a few more photos for his rotation flap records, not social media, as I was shaking from head to toe with excitement. I kept crying, from nowhere, I think my ballcock was jammed! I had the skin of a rhino and had healed well, where there had been an angry red bloodied line was now a narrow pink scar. He was a genius, he truly knew what he was doing, he had planned it, drawn on me, avoided chopping off my left arm, or anything else for that matter, and had done everything to ensure that I could still get into a bikini again, if I so wished.

It was time to say goodbye, for now, and he gave me a one-sided hug, something I had now perfected, and I didn't want to let him go. It just didn't seem enough to throw my clothes back on and just walk out of the room looking to high-five someone, so as my right side was my strongest, I hugged my Hero very tightly into me, to silently indicate my unending gratitude for what he had done, as I was now being passed back to oncology at the Leicester Royal Infirmary.

I whipped off the gown, put it in the wash-basket with a flourish, got dressed and neatly stacked my shopping basket back onto the rack. It was my final act of being tidy before I started the next stage. For the first time I stood topless, proudly. In all the fuss my headscarf and skull cap had come off in the process of trying to get dressed too quickly. My hands were shaking in the excitement as I struggled to get them back on. Darren stood watching me as I was trying to cover my very short covering of hair on my scalp. It was dark enough to see the outline of my hairline, but still ridiculously short, and as my hands shook and I tried for a third time to get everything in place, when he said, "No, keep it off Bear and walk out of here proud." So, I did.

We walked down the corridor between current and future patients and their families, as I was strutting my stuff and confident in the knowledge that I was going to be OK. I was back on life's catwalk. This was the first day of the rest of my life. As I strode down to the reception desk to get my next appointment, I wanted to high-five everyone, it was my turn after all. I wanted to shout out loud, "Yes, I'm bald, I still look like crap, but I am so happy." Each day I had felt that little bit better and I wanted to tell everyone there that if you fight, you actually have a chance of winning. I did notice the cool breeze across my now exposed head, but it felt wonderful. It felt bloody wonderful actually except my ears were freezing again! Nothing mattered any more, and as we walked proudly out of the building, we knew I had won. I had finally beaten the squatter, he was finally evicted. We returned to the car and I wanted to ring everyone at the same time, I garbled the news first to one, then to the other, talking, laughing, crying, the relief was palpable.

A few days later the usual buff coloured envelope with the usual typeface arrived, and that same feeling of dread came over me. It was the radiotherapy planning appointment set for Wednesday 16th May 2012. I had no idea what this involved as, in my joy over the last few days, I really hadn't had the thought to research it. I didn't know if it would hurt, if it would burn, if it would scar me. It was a laser beam for heaven's sake, would I smell like supermarket rotisserie chicken? When I did start to research it, all I would be told was, "This is the easy part."

Yet again we returned to the Leicester Royal Infirmary. The MDT (Planning Team) had decided on five weeks of daily radiotherapy. Wow, they had put me on the fast track to parole, but I was still confident, still recovering and ready to face anything. I attended the pre-assessment and was taught how to look after my breast and the skin as the laser beam is aimed at burning the tissue inside and up towards my armpit and would be a final internal flush to back up the work of the chemotherapy and warned me of the tiredness that came with it. I had to have a scan to work out the specifications for the radiotherapy beam, because it's not simply a case of sitting in front of the beam and being zapped in a general area, it's all a little more accurate than that.

So, into another gown I lay on the bed, which was slowly moved into the large metal tube. They moved me in slowly so I didn't panic but eventually all you could see were my feet with the technologist speaking to me through speakers. It is very claustrophobic and can be quite daunting, but I had faced worse. I had faced cancer for goodness sake, this was nothing. It was over, I came back out and they told me to sit on the side of the bed so they could work out where my breasts sat. The nurses read out a series of numbers to the senior oncologist and they dotted three places across my chest; one at the side of my left breast, one in the middle of my chest, and one to the side of my right breast. Then they told me I was going to have tattoos!

Now, I have lived a rich and varied life, and have burnt the candle in the middle as well at both ends, but I have never had the courage, or the desire, to have a tattoo. My upper body was bruised, battered, scarred and now they wanted me to have tattoos? Did I not have enough permanent reminders of what I had been through? The nurse's hand was shaking as I was told to lie back down and not move. I asked her not to press too hard as I didn't want some large serpent, or dragon, or some badly translated Chinese symbols. Instead they were the smallest blue dots, which would guide the positioning of the radiotherapy lasers over the next five weeks. I then opted for my appointments to be first thing in the morning, because I had to drive into Leicester every day and I wanted to get them over with so I could have the rest of the day to myself, and to sleep by the sounds of the side effects.

I was due to start Wednesday 30th May 2012 and they were due to finish Wednesday 4th July 2012. My end dates had become the goals I worked to and the countdown to freedom had started. It's what kept me going.

When I got home, I jumped in the shower, as I had been prodded, poked and drawn on again. I'd got hot and bothered and I just wanted to wash the hospital smell off me. While I was in the shower Darren came in to chat and, as I was feeling happier than I had done in a long time, as a joke, I pressed my boobs up against the cold shower doors to leave an imprint on the condensation. Darren saw me and laughed, while I stepped back in the shower to admire my work of art. Through the laughter and the steam I was a little surprised, "Gosh, they're low!" I said. Darren continued laughing and said, "I'm saying nothing," which was a wise and safe response.

When I got out the shower and looked down at myself, I could see that the marker pen had been washed off but the small blue dots of the tattoos remained. Again, I was confused, "Why are the tattoos so low? I thought they were going to put them where my breasts sat?" Again, Darren laughed but said nothing. Then a very loud penny dropped. Clang! That WAS where they sat! Gravity was taking over and things were heading south. As I dried myself I shrugged, inwardly. Do you know what, who gives a hoot where they hang? Who cares if one hangs lower than the other? Who cares if I have one, two or none? Who cares about the scarring? These were my boobs, they were part of me and we were healthy and cancer free. My life was back on track, I was eating cranberry cakes like there was no tomorrow and I finally had tattoos!

CHAPTER 20 – THE HEAT IS ON

It was the morning of Wednesday 30th May 2012. As Darren and I arrived at Leicester Royal Infirmary, we gave the pink breast cancer charity cranberry cakes to our newfound friend, the car park attendant. It turned out, in one of our many conversations, that he too was undergoing radiotherapy. We then headed for the Osborne Building, but this time I was destined for the ground floor, as I had been effectively moved out of the Chemotherapy Suite. This meant, of course, that I was going to miss all the familiar faces.

We headed for the Radiotherapy Suite, which was to be my new home for the next five weeks. It was more like a "normal" waiting room. Despite there being one or two ladies in headscarves, you couldn't tell amongst the others who was the patient and who was the support. Beds were being wheeled in and out with patients from the hospital wards for their appointments and some did not look well at all. I was starting to feel like a fraud sitting there, as my hair had started to slowly show signs of growing back, and despite my swarthy skin and wonky breasts, I was in recovery. But then I had to check in with myself, I did deserve to be there. For once, this was about me. Although I had been told the operations were a success, my treatment was not yet over and I still needed medical intervention. As we waited, we were asked by friendly volunteers if we wanted tea or coffee, and I felt I could get used to spending my days here.

We could see on a board that the five radiation machines had been named after five different areas in Leicestershire, and I was designated "Bosworth." My name was called and I was given a complicated set of instructions of where to go, left here, through the doors, turn right…but I'd stopped listening. I had too many other things running through my head. I soon discovered though that I should have listened as this place was huge and a bit of a maze. Eventually we saw signs for Bosworth, and we headed for another waiting room. My mind was racing and I found myself staring at the other people waiting to see if they were as petrified as I was. The main question running through my head was, "Is this going to hurt?"

A male nurse appeared from a corridor with a patient and they said their goodbyes. I looked at her closely to see if she was distressed or in pain, but she looked fine. Not ruffled, not upset, and more importantly, not burnt! The nurse then turned to me and ran through my form to double-check it was me. I was hoping for the "Any distinguishing marks?" question so I could tell him I had scars on my breast and now had a series of tattoos around my waist. OK, I exaggerate, they weren't that low, but they were lower than a pert young woman's breasts should be, if you know what I mean.

I said goodbye to Darren through a gulp and the nurse walked with me along a very clinical corridor with radiation signs everywhere, and warning signs for "Keep Clear." I felt like I'd fallen into some sort of spy movie and was being led down to some top-secret bunker. As we turned the corner I was taken aback by a huge and clearly, extremely expensive machine surrounded by four members of staff. They introduced themselves but I heard none of their names as I took in the machine, the bed and saw my name on a screen next to a series of numbers. I was told to gown up, and you'd think after all these months I'd have mastered it by now, but behind the screen I struggled with the ribbons nervously, more so knowing people were waiting for me. It's ironic really that they provide you with privacy at every turn, but at any minute my tattooed boobs would be on display to half a dozen members of staff. Again!

I reappeared wearing the gown, my trousers and my shoes, then tried to nimbly leap onto the bed with no effort, but did my usual puffing and panting as I climbed in a very undignified way onto the bed, trying to hold my gown closed and tearing the paper sheet as I went. The nurses could see my dilemma and stepped in to help, more hands trying to keep the gown shut as I fidgeted on the bed to get a good position. I lay back, missed the pillow, more fidgeting, and they adjusted the bed to the correct height. I had to keep my head fairly flat on the bed and they put a roll underneath my knees – a fabric one not a Swiss one! My left arm was raised and I had to tuck it behind my head. This was remarkably comfortable, because like a good girl, I had been doing my exercises to prevent any "cording" as I was still healing internally. This is why it is so important to do the exercises. I could miss a day of exercising and could really feel the pull the next day. Just keep doing them as it does pay off in the end. It's a simple ten minutes out of your day but a huge gain in your life.

I was really comfortable when my gown was opened to reveal my left breast and they commented on how very neat the surgeon had been. I told them that the operation was only five weeks ago and they were amazed at the rate of my healing. After my tattoos had been located, perhaps a little bit further down than they were expecting, the machine was lined up and I was told to lie perfectly still and not move a muscle.

Of course, when you're told not to move a muscle, you want to twitch and fidget like mad, but I concentrated hard on not moving because the sooner this was over and done with, the better. My personal details were checked again and then came a series of numbers and coordinates, which were discussed across me as they checked, double checked and triple checked, then they were signed off. The machine was moved into position above me, almost like a huge X-ray machine, and again they told me not to move a muscle as they lined up the laser beams to my tattoos. Then, they legged it! Not quite running out the room, but not far off! They had to leave the area but told me not to worry, as they would be monitoring me closely on the screen. So…they had gone and I was there in a room full of radiation?

I had to look to my right, away from the beam, but I could still see it out of the corner of my eye. There was a loud beeping sound and then the beam shot directly at my breast. I could hear it, see it, but couldn't feel anything. I lay waiting for it to warm up but after another loud series of beeps the beam stopped and they all came back into the room. I had felt nothing. A further discussion of dimensions took place and the machine was moved to my right hand side at an angle and was aimed directly into my armpit. They were covering all areas. Again, they left the room and the process started all over again. After the final beep, they all came back in, moved the machine away and covered me up. Considering the predicament of my situation, and the exposure of such a personal area, they were all terribly kind and very respectful. I had to lie still while they altered the height of the bed again and took away my knee raiser. They helped me get off the bed and I could get dressed behind the curtain, suggesting that I kept the gown and bring it along to my daily appointments. This would at least give me the opportunity to spend some quality time at home learning how to tie the blinking thing properly. Maybe I could record an online course in "How to Tie Your Hospital Gown with Ease" and post it on the internet! The nurse then led me back to reception where I found Darren flicking through a dog-eared magazine. He was not expecting me back after a speedy 15 minutes and to look so relaxed.

So, this was to be my daily routine for the next five weeks. They had given me weekends off. By day three, I calculated that the time it took me to get undressed, gowned up, on the bed, throttling myself with the gown, the treatment, closing the gown, struggling to sit up without throttling myself again, taking the gown off to get dressed, I suggested that if it didn't offend anyone, maybe I should forget the gown all together because it was more trouble than it was worth. Taking into consideration there were a couple of young male nurses in there, I was well aware that they saw boobs all day long in their line of work. I had lower than usual tattoos and I was no pin up girl! They agreed that if I felt confident enough they were happy to go along with it as some ladies were not comfortable with the complete exposure before and after the treatment. I felt it would speed up the process, and I wasn't sure why it was necessary to cover my boobs if they were going to be on display for the treatment anyway! And let's face it, the greyish-blue colour of the gown matched my skin tone, so it was hard to tell whether I was wearing it anyway.

As I saw the same medics, day in and day out, the conversations became more familiar and I was soon chatting about what their children were doing, who had won at bowling the night before and what they were seeing at the cinema. Equally, they were finding out about me, and when I told them that my sister Sarah and I were taking part in the Cancer Research Race For Life at Bath University in a few days' time they were shocked. One of them said, "But you're only seven weeks out of surgery!" "I know," I said, "but I can't wait another year before I put something back into the system that has saved my life." They were pleased and supportive but also warned me that the radiotherapy can cause extreme tiredness and that I had to pace myself. This surprised me, because I was nearly halfway through the process and couldn't actually feel anything happening, apart from the after effects. These consisted of a dry scaly boob and crispy nipple, nice, enlarged pores on the breast and a slobbering snorting awakening after falling asleep on the "poorly chair" in the afternoon after watching some daytime TV, thanks to the chemotherapy!

So, two weeks into the treatment, Darren, Tom and I drove down to Bath to stay with Sarah and Bruce. We went shopping for our pink items. We had set a sponsorship target of £500, but this was achieved within a week after Darren donated the target. So we increased it to £2000, but our continued support of sponsorship raised over!

The excitement had overtaken any feelings of doubt, and at no point did I think, "I'm really not sure I can do this!" I was now so determined that if it took me a week to get round the course, then it would take me a week. I was going to cross that finishing line, no matter what. We had a hearty breakfast, and Sarah decided that we should drop the roof on her two-seater convertible, with our backup team in the other car. My hair was still frighteningly short so I wore my pink cap to match my pink feather boa, sunglasses, jacket, t-shirt, earrings, plastic jewellery, and of course, the pink pig hand puppets – it's what all the top athletes wear, in case you were wondering. As we drove onto the campus the car park attendant saw us in our pink attire and pointed us in the direction of a smaller, closer car park. When we told him, foolishly, that we were taking part in the race (as if he hadn't realised), he pointed out that we deserved to park in the VIP car park for looking so amazing. Doesn't happen everyday, so we took that as a compliment.

We walked down to the course and Sarah, who had taken part in a couple of these events in previous years, told me of the mixed feelings I would have. Although there is a great atmosphere of fun, happiness and laughter, it is closely matched by the feelings of immense sadness as you read the signs on people's backs and are reminded of the real reason you are there. But we were all there for the same purpose, to raise much-needed funds to make it possible for less people to die in vain. This wasn't just about me.

Darren, Bruce, Tom and my mum all parked in the main car park (miles away, no VIP parking) in Bruce's support vehicle. As we turned into the field where everyone congregates, we were met by a sea of pink, tutus, wigs, hats, streamers, leggings, you name it, it was in pink, and the noise, the chattering, the laughter, and the shouting and singing. There were individuals, teams, people posing for photos, dogs taking part (with owners of course) and more ladies squeezed into pink Lycra than you could shake a stick at! A local DJ makes ridiculous and corny jokes, all to put you at your ease, and then you take part in a Zumba workout to get warmed up. This brought back emotional memories for me as this was where my cancer journey had begun, all those months before. If it hadn't been for Zumba and the collision, I would never have discovered my lump, and I may not be here now. It was strange to think what I had been through in the past year. Who would have thought I would then be standing there in a pink field? The instructor shouted out instructions, one of which included "Come on girls, swing your hair!" Whoa, hang on, look around you. But I laughed and shouted at Sarah, above the loud music, "What hair?"

We were then called to take our positions depending on ability: runners, joggers and walkers. The heat was on. There was no point pretending, we were going to walk it. We had drink rations which Sarah popped into her pink emergency bag, in case I needed some help along the way, as the route took us away from the crowd of supporters and through a couple of fields, where the only company would be fellow pink ladies and a herd or two of cows and their excrement! We waved at the supporters as we shuffled along in the crowd of fellow walkers, and passed under the start line timer. We didn't stroll, but kept up a decent and steady pace, with Sarah reassuring me that anytime I wanted to stop I could. But never once did she say "and if you want to drop out if it's too much, then we can." She knew we were on a mission and it was driven by our determination.

Soon after starting, I re-discovered that another side effect I had obtained was wheezing, and as I concentrated on getting as much oxygen into my rasping chest as I could, I could hear Sarah giving me an update on our progress, "1km completed Clare Bear. Are you OK?" At 3km I had a slight coughing fit which concerned others, but waving them on with an "I'm fine" comment, I was determined not to stop, so Sarah slowed the pace right down and we carried on. I was now so far into this that I was sure that if I had to finish this crawling on my hands on knees, that's what I'd do. Suddenly, without realising it, because you are so caught up with the emotional rollercoaster of reading other people's signs, taking part in memory of parents, grandparents, family and friends, we were near the end. It occurred to me that if things had gone differently, maybe my name would be on some of these signs. But, instead, I was now approaching the final stretch and could hear the buzz and the cheers of the well-wishers in the distance beyond the trees, with the echo of the DJ. Sarah suggested that in our achievement we should link arms and run the last few meters to get under the banner. For me, this was the last middle finger up gesture to the squatter who had arrived without an invitation, who had taken up residency, who had been found squatting nine months previously and who had pushed me to the limits of my health.

The emotion of it all was starting to catch up with me. It had been an emotional few miles and my physical struggle was getting weirdly easier as my adrenalin was pushing me on. I had managed to overtake people and I was still undergoing treatment. Was this the turning point of my health? Was I finally getting better? I felt like I was leaving cancer behind and I felt like I was finally winning. This was my own personal race nearly completed. My motto, "Tomorrow I will feel a little bit better" had worked.

As we "ran" towards the finishing line we could just make out Bruce and his camera in the crowd, taking action shots of us as we ran past. The best picture he managed to get was Sarah and me jogging under the banner, linked together, supporting each other through this terrible journey, but successfully crossing the finishing line, with the sign that was safety pinned to my back, telling the whole world that I was taking part as a thank you to all those people who had helped to save my life. Even though the clock above our heads showed the time, we calculated that we had managed it in just under an hour, because some time had passed before we had got near to the start line as so many people were taking part.

I was exhausted, wheezing, but I was on a high. We received a goody bag, but most importantly our finisher's medals! This meant more than just the Race For Life. This felt like a medal of survival. I whipped the cap from my sweaty, baldy head, not caring who saw me. This was another place I could fit in and be accepted. As I threw the ribbon over my head the emotion of the day overwhelmed me and Sarah threw her arms around me in a celebratory, comforting hug. Words of congratulations were ringing in my ears and all I could feel was her love and her warmth. I was going to be OK. This was the final reassurance.

After lots of photos, including a "We Did It" snap from one of the sponsors of the day, Heart FM, we returned to the car. Everyone was leaving at the same time and so we sat in a long queue of traffic. This gave us time to entertain passing children, and adults, with our pink pig glove puppets. When we eventually got back to the house, family and a few friends sat around enjoying a "pink" lunch that Sarah had arranged. Then it was quick shower, back in the car and home. An exhausting day, physically and emotionally, but I wore my medal all the way home. I had earned it!

CHAPTER 21 – KNIGHT OF ONCOLOGY

On the Monday morning I was back at the Radiotherapy Suite. I would usually whip everything off whilst talking to the nurses, but this time, I disappeared behind the curtain and came out topless, but wearing my Race For Life medal! "Yay!" they all cheered in unison. Not because I was topless but because I was wearing my medal may I add! Well I think that's why they were cheering? Congratulations rang around the room, but unfortunately I wasn't allowed to keep it on during the treatment, although one of the nurses popped it back over my head as soon as it was over.

After about two weeks of daily treatment I had noticed that my breast was starting to get very sore, dry and tender to touch. I had been smothering it daily in aqueous cream but it wasn't helping. I was due for my "Treat and Review," which sadly doesn't mean that someone brings you a tub of ice cream and a spoon and then asks what your concerns are as you are swinging your legs on the bed. Instead, a specialist nurse assesses how the radiotherapy is progressing. I explained my concerns and she decided to apply some cream pads, which meant I was lapped in cream with the protective pads taped to me. The pads protected the breast from drying out any further so that the treatment could continue, and they prevented the skin from rubbing on my underwear which could be irritating and painful and also stopped the dry skin from cracking and bleeding (yet again, I hope you're not eating).

So, if you are experiencing the same problem, keep applying the cream as much as you need to. If you are alone then give the area some air! I'm certainly not suggesting you should get your chest out at a dinner party! Not unless you really want to draw attention to yourself.

My next problem raised was the wheezing. This was not getting any better. A radiologist checked my "scan" proofs and suggested it was very likely that the radiation was catching the top of my left lung. Unfortunately this was not repairable, it would permanently scar and treatment could not be stopped. I had opted from the start that to get rid of cancer I would take any consequences, so this was to be one of them and the problem continues where I wheeze and can get a bit breathless. Usually when walking uphill so I desperately try to avoid this. I had more cream pump dispensers, tubes of cream, clear tape and pads than the hospital.

By the time of my next "Treat and Review' my breast was recovering well even though I was still having daily

Radiotherapy. With the onset of the side effects it was decided that I should see an oncologist. After I'd "gowned-up" I waited for the oncologist to arrive. I had not been seen by this one before. When we met, she bore an uncanny resemblance to Miss Marple! She checked me over but was happy for me to continue the treatment. I told her that I was now looking forward to the date they gave me the all clear and that it couldn't come soon enough. It was my goal. She dropped a bit of a bombshell by telling me, "We never give you the all-clear dear!" What?

After nearly five weeks of radiotherapy I had an outline of an angled brown box across my breast. Little did I know it had burned straight through to my back as well. It wasn't painful, just tender to the touch and sometimes slightly itched.

It was now 4th July 2012. Oddly, by the end of the fifth week of treatment, I felt an overwhelming sadness that the people I had grown so close to, and with whom I had developed a friendship, would no longer be in my life. My routine of getting home exhausted, trying to stay awake on the settee, whilst reading *Fifty Shades of Grey* with my boob hanging out and my baldy head exposed, kept me going!

I had grown particularly fond of one nurse in the radiotherapy team, as I felt she really took extra special time to speak to me, to give me advice and to ask about my welfare. Just one of those people you bond with. I never once moaned and she could see my determination to get through this. On my last day of treatment I arrived at the hospital alone. My friends had volunteered to go with me, and on a couple of occasions one friend had accompanied me. The hours of the radiotherapy appointments meant that she was the most flexible and she worked the journey into her work schedule. My cousin Neil had offered at times to take me, but he was keeping an eye on my Dad, as I wasn't well enough to be around him with his COPD. But this was my last day and I was fine.

I took in a box of cranberry cakes for each of the team who had cared for me and attached a "thank you" note. My favourite nurse wasn't around but I left some at the reception desk for her. I felt sad that I hadn't been able to see her face to face and foolish that I had just assumed she would always be at the hospital whenever I was. Everyone sent me on my way with their best wishes and kind words and I headed off to see my Oncologist. I felt quite sad but as I exited through the double doors I saw my favourite nurse coming through at the same time. Both our faces lit up and we greeted each other like old friends. I explained that I had completed my last treatment and that there was a small package waiting for her with a "thank you" card to the team. I felt a little nervous and she stepped forward and hugged me, "Well done to you," she said. I could have cried. I seemed to spend most of my time at the hospital being emotional. I told her that I was still waiting for my final release and said, "If I don't get it, I will be back." She replied, "No, you won't!" And we parted ways.

I hoped that she had headed straight for the package and saw the card, which read:

To My Radiotherapy Gang,

Thank you for all your care and attention to finish my breast cancer treatment. You have all made it so much easier to come in everyday and you probably do not realise the impact your good work has. I can hopefully get back to normal now. My support team express their thanks in returning me to them and I cannot thank you enough. Keep up the good work!

I then carried on to see the oncologist and took a seat in the waiting room. My hair was now of such a length that I wore the scarves less and less as they would make my head really hot, bearing in mind it was now the summer. It was now growing back in the places it should return to, except for the downstairs region. For some reason that was a bit patchy! I could feel a woman constantly staring at me and I kept thinking, "Oh no, she is looking at my baldy head." I was now wearing headbands and as I turned to look at her she said hello. I returned the greeting and vaguely recognised her. She then said that she had seen me at Glenfield Hospital and recognised me from my eyes. I thought she'd said "arse" and we both laughed. I explained that this should be the last time I was at the hospital and she asked me, "Where's your husband today?"

"I don't have one," I said.

"Oh that's sad. So who is the tall man I have seen you at Glenfield with?"

I explained that it was Darren and that we were not married. Saying that out loud made me sound quite lonely and made me realise that nothing had changed. I said I was fine being there on my own. But now, when I think back on it, I was not fine on my own. I should have gone out the same way I went in. This was my last day of treatment, hopefully forever, but I'd been stubborn, and sure of myself, and had rejected all offers of help. Darren was working and I had needed to do this last stretch on my own. But, in many ways, I did need this time alone, to say my goodbyes and to reflect on what had happened over the last few months, the outcome I'd had, and how close it had come to being different. I needed the time to regain my focus and not be concerned with checking that the person with me was OK. My name was called and I wished the Glenfield lady all the best as I leapt to my feet.

I was excited to see the oncologist as I wanted him to be as thrilled as I was about how far I had come. The charity cranberry cakes were selling and raising money, I had completed my first, and not my last Race For Life, and I was generally well, still in recovery, but feeling better than I had for a long time. Each day, as I had always told myself, that tomorrow I would feel a little bit better. I entered the room, and yes, you guessed it, gowned up! I had finally learnt that it was best to dress for the occasion and have the ability to take less and less off so I wasn't messing about with zips and buttons, but for heaven's sake, I had still not got the hang of these three-ribboned gowns.

As the oncologist came into the room, I gave him a big confident smile as he firmly shook my hand. Both he and the nurse agreed that I was looking well and that on inspection my breast was recovering at a good rate. This was going to be my last chance to say anything to the team who had saved my life. Slightly choked, I told him that I could never thank him enough for all he had done, and that the same went for all the nurses and the rest of the team involved. He modestly shrugged it off, and told me that I was free to go and that he would see me in a year in a very casual un-panicked manner. At the end of the month I would see the surgeon again and this passing from one to the other would continue for the foreseeable future. My Knight of Oncology had other people to save and he would work just as hard for them as he had worked hard for me, another real life Angel.

I had a gift and a card for him too and I had written:

I cannot thank you enough and all of the medical team in getting me through my battle with breast cancer. The care and attention I have received is amazing. I can now return to my role of daughter, sister, mother, girlfriend and work colleague, knowing I had the best of care. It takes special people to care for special people.

I updated him on all the fundraising. The cake sales had raised a staggering £37,000, and Sarah and I had also added £2,000 to this amount from the Race For Life sponsorship. All in aid of charity. He was thrilled and told me to keep up the good work. My treatment was complete, except for the Tamoxifen tablet I would be taking on a daily basis for the next five years. Its aim was to shut down my ovaries and to stop me from producing oestrogen which my cancer fed from and to kick me into early menopause. Lovely but not quite what I expected. As it kicked me into menopause it kicked me into hot sweats. It's like being hit by a blow torch. Tom would frequently be in hysterics as I would tell him to get away from me before I ignited!

So, I was finished and released. I shook his hand for what felt like the last time and he left the room. I removed the gown off, screwed it up into a ball and threw it hard into the laundry basket at the end of the examining bed. Hopefully, I'll never wear you again and struggle to tie you up, I thought and that was it. I dressed and unlocked the door. As I walked through the waiting room I felt like I should be saying to everyone "Bye then!" Instead, I walked out of the Radiotherapy Suite and quietly along the corridor. I felt slightly overwhelmed as I passed the staircase which led to the Chemotherapy Suite. I remembered all too clearly all the times I had struggled on the staircase and Darren had to lift me to help me get up them. In reality I was always hoping that someone would say if you can't make it just leave it, but I knew I was destined for that suite.

Seeing the staircase reminded me of the weakness brought on by the chemotherapy and how far I had now come. I was now walking further than the end of my drive! My usual stubborn self had always refused to take the lift, "If I can't walk up the stairs, it's a sad day," I'd say. Boy did I struggle, but I always congratulated myself on getting the much-needed exercise. It was all so clear in my mind, remembering how I had felt. Shouldn't I had left to a fanfare and fireworks, running hand in hand with Gerard Butler, or was I just so grateful that they had all helped me? I was not just an NHS number. I had been their much cared for patient and now they were all too busy helping others to say their goodbyes.

I walked out of the hospital and out of the grounds, and I wondered what on earth I was going to do now. In fact, what was I going to do next week? Where would I go? Has it really gone? What if this cancer comes back and no one is around to check it or detect it? Moving to annual appointments seemed such a long way away. But, it was down to me now. I was no expert, and how would I know? What would I look for? Does it come back the same? The relief and jubilation at leaving the hospital was also mixed with a slight air of panic as this was all I had known for the past year and I hadn't even made it to the car park!

CHAPTER 22 – GETTING IT OFF MY CHEST

My next appointment was set for the 31st July 2012 to see the surgeon at Glenfield and for what I hoped would be an opportunity for him to tell me how brilliant I was. I wanted someone to tell me what a good girl I had been for recovering from this dreadful disease. Despite not telling me this, the meeting went well and I had one last referral to oncology on 5th August 2012 when I would be released and placed into the annual appointment system. It was around this time that my repeat cervical smear test was due. This in itself had been a bit of a saga, with it all starting in July 2010, and the results came back as normal! Finally, fate really was on my side these days. Bit by bit, I was getting confirmation, from all quarters, that I was cancer free.

With all this positivity, it seemed strange to admit that I was suddenly feeling a little lost, a bit alone. I had undergone nine months of constant medical attention, sometimes daily, and now suddenly I had no medical personnel visiting me, no hospital appointments, no GP check-ups and no more treatments to undergo. I was back in the real, healthy world and I would need time to become accustomed to it. I don't want this to come across as some sort of attention seeking sob-story, but I was experiencing feelings of abandonment. I would lie in bed wondering if they had just erased my name off the system so I would be forgotten. It began to play on my mind constantly. I was becoming paranoid about the simplest of things. My breasts didn't feel the same any more. Don't forget, we had been quite close since my early teens as an early developer and now I had to get to know them again. As the nerves inside were repairing themselves they would send shooting pains across my chest and I would have a few hours worrying that maybe the cancer was reforming. As the days became weeks I became more and more scared.

I didn't know what signs to look out for. Let's face it, I hadn't felt in the slightest bit ill when I'd been diagnosed the year before, so how on earth was I going to know there was a new problem? But rather than make a fuss, I played the martyr and decided to harbour all these feelings of terror under the surface so no-one else would know or start to worry. I certainly didn't want to start becoming a nuisance at the hospital and ring them every time I felt a twinge. I didn't want them to answer my call and roll their eyes mouthing to each other "It's her again!" So, I sat down with my folder of leaflets and letters and telephoned Coping With Cancer. It didn't matter that the cancer was now in the past tense. I had "coped" with cancer and they are there for you, your family and anyone connected with cancer. During the call, which of course I started with a series of "Really sorry to bother you but..." and "I don't want to waste anyone's time but..." a home visit was arranged.

A few days later, ironically a day I thought I was feeling strong and well, a lady from Coping With Cancer arrived and we sat down with a cup of tea. She asked me to explain the journey I had been on, and I started talking. I talked and talked and talked, I barely stopped for breath. I found myself off-loading the last year to this complete stranger and then, right on cue, the tears made their appearance. I sniffed my way through apologies but she reassured me and when I had calmed down she told me that they were there to help me through this. She said I should have contacted them immediately on diagnosis because apart from the emotional support, they can also offer financial advice. It had never occurred to me that I could have applied for help with this, when money had become quite stretched while I tried to balance work, home life and treatment. She was staggered that I had shouldered all this along with the cancer. I told her I had continued to work, albeit in between chemotherapy treatments, and I had kept up with my mortgage payments and household bills, albeit with the occasional financial boost from Darren and my family. But generally, my independent spirit had won the day, and I had kept everything afloat. I was too proud, and maybe I should have sought help earlier, but I had coped and I had managed. Now I needed help from a different quarter, I needed some emotional guidance and she was there to help me find my way.

She made arrangements for me to visit the centre and meet one of the counsellors, and blimey did he get both barrels! I thought the sobbing with her was bad enough, but he got the lot and I found it quite cathartic. We got to the root of the problems and fears in no time, which in many ways was better, rather than taking weeks and weeks of sessions. By the third session I was casually leaning back in the armchair, balancing a cup of tea on my knee, telling *him* the way forward. At the end of the session he admitted that he didn't think there was anything else he could do for me because I seemed to be already sorted and mentally in the right place for once in my life! He admitted that it was unusual to be sorted so quickly and didn't feel he had done enough, but bless him, he had been in the right place at the right time for me and he had helped me immensely. I was back on track. I had also been offered some Reiki treatment but this was cancelled as my counselling had finished. Therapists volunteer to perform this treatment on cancer patients and I think this is a lovely gesture.

So now I had embarked on another journey, the one of recovery. Sometimes I felt quite low, and it was difficult to get this across to people because it seemed ungrateful to moan as I had finished my treatment, so what was my problem? As the treatment had finished, people can presume you are cured and back to normal. The ones that were closest to me knew there was something awry as I wasn't the same person as before. I knew I was different, I had been through a life-changing event, I was battered, scarred, tired, aching, sometimes snappy, internally repairing, had restricted movement and I was physically and emotionally different, I was a bit of a mess. So Darren and I decided to do one of the things that I was desperate to do throughout treatment. Stand at the front of the sea, with my arms held up to the sky and breathe in the sea air. So we headed off to Wales and that's exactly what we did! I stood at the furthest point out to the sea and I inhaled. The fresh air of life.

Each night I promised myself that tomorrow I would feel a

little bit better, but actually months were going by and I wasn't. I didn't get it. What was happening now? It was November 2012 and one afternoon I got back from work to a warm centrally heated house, but needed to keep my coat on. I was frozen to the core. I would sit on the settee and my head would fall forward and I would sleep, soundly. I felt like I had the flu, but oddly, only down my left hand side, and my daily bodily functions were all over the place too. I would wake up with a snort and see Tom wandering about in shorts and a tee shirt while I still sat huddled in my coat asking him to turn the heating up. This was not right!

So, it was time for another doctor's appointment. I explained my symptoms and he said that I needed to get a blood test immediately because this had all the hallmarks of bone cancer! What? Had the chemotherapy not wiped just about everything out of me and now you're telling me I might have bone cancer? Can you survive bone cancer? Would this terrible nightmare ever end? I numbly left his office and walked to the Health Centre with a blood test form marked "Urgent" and sat in the waiting room. Had I not seen this form before? Had I really come this far just to fall at the final hurdle after all?

I knew the phlebotomist quite well now and as she searched my chemotherapy scarred arm in the hope that a vein would miraculously make an appearance, I discussed the possibilities with her. She was supportive and positive and tried to alleviate the obvious fears the thoughtless doctor had put in my head. I left with my arm covered in clear tape and rang Darren who met me at home. After a bit more of a rant I settled down in front of my computer and typed in "bone cancer." Bit of advice, don't do that, ever. Whatever illness you investigate you seem to have it. The test had been on the Thursday and I wouldn't get my results back until the Monday, so I envisaged a few days of sleepless nights and frantic days. On the Friday, trying unsuccessfully to keep myself occupied, I rang the surgery to ask how soon my results would be in on Monday.

"Miss Collins," she said, "We have been trying to contact you all day. The lab rang us on receiving your bloods. Can you get back to the surgery within the hour?" Now, if you can get to see a doctor at 4pm on a Friday this cannot be good news. They had been in receipt of my blood less than 24 hours and I had to go back? This was not good. This was not good at all. I rang Darren, "I'm on my way Bear," he said.

As we sat in the waiting room every poster and leaflet that my eyes rested on dealt with cancer. This was definitely a sign it was back. In fact, it had never left me. It had tricked me into believing I was free but it had just taken up residence somewhere else. Laughing at me that my back was turned for a second and it had returned with its suitcase, uninvited again. Since my last hospital appointment, all those twinges and spasms I had bravely ignored were all signs to something wrong and I had missed every single one of them. I had left it far too late. I had fooled myself into believing that I was free of it, and this was the cruellest joke of all.

Finally, my name flashed up on the board and Darren grabbed my sweaty hand and we walked down to the doctor's office. I sat in the chair, dry mouthed and shaking and could feel the colour drain from my face. But to be honest, this wasn't unusual, as the aggressive chemotherapy had left me with a pale colour at the best of times. This was a different doctor to the one who delivered the earth-shattering news the day before, and he explained each stage of the blood tests in detail which just seemed to be taking forever Here I was again, searching the face of the news-giver, looking for any sign of regret, sorrow, pity. Eventually, he got to the point, "Anaemia – Clear." He then looked at me properly for the first time, and I dread to think what either of us looked like because he leant forward to me and asked, "Are you OK?"

"Can you just tell me if I have bone cancer please," I croaked, through my dry mouth. He looked at me, amazed, "What? Why do you think you have bone cancer?"

"Because that is what I am being tested for." I replied.

"No, no," he said, "It's your thyroid. It's off the scale. It's in amber alert. You have hypothyroidism."

"What? So it's not cancer?"

He reassured me that it absolutely wasn't. I took in the longest breath as Darren nearly fell forward off his chair. Who cared what it was? Who cared what they'd found? It wasn't cancer! So, another breath and then more questions, "My thyroid?" It was damaged, probably a likely consequence of the radiotherapy. Another side effect I would have to cope with. Something else to investigate now. What does your thyroid do? Why have I got one? Why do we not all know this?

My Friday evening was spent on the internet learning all there was to know about the thyroid and its function in the body as I deleted "bone cancer" out of my favourites. I'm an expert on it now, ask me anything! The thyroid keeps all your organs in order, and because mine was damaged, my organs, my bodily functions and my internal thermometer were all over the place and slowly coming to a halt. Blimey, can you imagine reading my doctors notes! So, another daily tablet of Levothyroxine was prescribed, and unlike the others, which I would be able to stop taking over time, because my thyroid was now damaged, I would have to take this tablet for life. I could update family on the next lot of news and felt like I was getting it off my chest whilst desperately hoping that would be it.

HAVING A BAD HAIR DAY

CHAPTER 23 – UNEXPECTED LOSSES

By Christmas 2012 I was back on track, so I thought, after I'd been on the counselling sessions. I still wasn't 100%, but I was closer to that number than I had been for a long, long time. With the help of the daily Levothyroxine tablet, my organs were back doing what they did best! I was looking forward to Christmas as always, as the year before I was undergoing chemotherapy, and this one was going to be a good one. It was always the reminder that I would not see another Christmas, being diagnosed in the September and watching Christmas decorations being put up everywhere. But I was here. I had survived.

My parents and Darren arrived to spend Christmas Day with

Tom and me, so after serving mince pies and cups of tea, and my annual, well-earned, much-awaited sherry, we started to open presents. A couple of weeks before, my cousin Neil had visited to see how I was recovering. Neil was my dad's nephew, born and raised in Glasgow and had come to live with my parents when he was 18. He lived with them for two years after finding work, then moved on and became very successful in his family life and career. He had been a great support constantly reminding me that I should never feel alone and he was always there for transport help getting to and from the hospital if I needed it. Whenever I saw him he would always give me a few bottles of shower gel which didn't cause an allergic reaction on my skin. I was still very tender and my skin was adjusting. Simple, thoughtful things. That was Neil.

It was now about 11am and all the presents had been opened when my dad's mobile phone rang. He looked at the screen and told us it was Neil. I walked over to my dad's chair and mouthed, "When you're finished, can I talk to him?" But as my dad listened it was clear by the look on his face that there was something terribly wrong. It wasn't Neil but his son. Neil had passed away Christmas morning from a massive heart attack. We were devastated. He had always been there, as much as he was a cousin, he was more like an uncle as he was closer in age to my parents. He had seen me through cancer, he had winked his support from across the room, he had hugged me in his big bear like way to tell me everything would be fine and he had given advice to Tom for university and a career. None of us had been able to help him. He had gone. He is still sorely missed by all the family and always will be.

Between Christmas and New Year my good friend who had been an adviser on my treatment, someone who had been on hand with advice when I needed it and a huge support, asked if I would like to join her on Trek Peru for Breast Cancer Care in the following May. Peru, isn't that in South America? Isn't that where Paddington Bear came from? I'd read all his books, as a child, you understand. Normally, I'd have come up with a thousand excuses for not going. Why not add this to my CV of life? How could I say no? I had no good reason to say no! I had visited about 17 countries so why not include this one? I knew I still wasn't fully recovered, but not only would it give me something to aim for, but also I could do this when so many others couldn't. I had no excuse and I had five months to prepare! Five short months to get this sorry excuse for a body into shape! So we signed up, and started the process of arranging a sponsorship campaign. We had a huge boost early on with her employers pledging a whopping £10,000 to get us started! What an incentive.

In the midst of my "training" I had another cervical smear test in February 2013, where the results back were normal. I was on a roll. Nothing could go wrong now. All I had to do was get through a third test successfully and I would be back to the two year system for testing. On 8th March 2013 I was due for my first "cancer free" surveillance mammogram. I was back to being topless and squished and squashed in all directions for the test. But I didn't care. They were monitoring me and my results read: "no evidence of breast cancer at this time." It could only get better and better.

This same month took me and nine of my friends off for a well-earned break in a barn conversion in Matlock, Derbyshire. It was a weekend of laughter, food and drink and I was beginning to feel like my life was coming back.

In April 2013, Darren, my dad and I visited Belfast for my cousin's wedding. I'd never been to Northern Ireland before and it was stunning. The scenery was breathtaking, the weather was gorgeous and the bride was beautiful. It was a friendly, warm, joyous occasion and I could relax and enjoy myself for the first time in months. Her wedding was superb. The day we were due to fly home I took a call from the emergency vet's again in Coventry. My cat, Clawdia, had been hit that morning by a car and a kind couple who witnessed the accident picked her up out of the road, wrapped her in a car blanket and took her in. A bit like history repeating itself with Louis. The vet told me that the outlook was not good and that I needed to come and see her. Through tears I explained that I was in Northern Ireland and due to fly back that day. What an ending to a wonderful weekend.

Clawdia was more than a cat to me, she was my pal. I had rescued her when I was going through chemotherapy and she had enlightened us all. She was full of character and cheek. She would tap the window with her claws to get back in and when I had been at my darkest throughout the cancer she had never failed to raise a smile with her antics. Maybe her role was to get me though the cancer and it was now my turn to comfort her. As soon as we landed we drove straight to the animal hospital and they took me through to her. Although I knew that she instantly recognised me, she was a mess. We were a mess. I asked the vet her honest opinion of what I was to do and she kindly told me to go home, have a cup of tea and think about what I wanted to do. I had given Clawdia a comforting stroke, told her how much I loved her and we left.

Our journey home took approximately 15 minutes and as we pulled up I got the call. She had passed away. It was almost as if she had hung on so I could say goodbye to her. After a time, when I hoped I had got most of my tears out, we drove back to Coventry to wrap her in her favourite blanket and so that I could say my last goodbyes. We were all devastated. She wasn't even two, but she had lived her life fast and died young, squeezing all those years of fun and life into two short years and helping me to recover. I had rescued her, yet she had rescued me too.

Rest in Peace Neil x

Goodnight Clawdia x

CHAPTER 24 – PLEASE LOOK AFTER "BEAR", THANK YOU

We had signed up for Trek Peru and I knew I had to start training. Deep in the back of my mind I kept wondering if I could honestly get this battered body back into some sort of reasonable shape so that I could walk to Machu Picchu. I would laugh hysterically at myself, "Of course I can!" I signed up to the local gym so I could climb into a swimsuit and clock up a few lengths and also step bravely on the treadmill. This was going to be easy.

The first swim was terrible. After one length I hung onto the side of the pool and considered plucking up the energy to haul myself out and get back into the safety of the changing room. My arms ached and weighed a thousand tonnes and my chest was tight and sore and was restricting my breathing, which was coming out as a pitiful wheeze. OK, maybe I needed to have a sterner word with myself because this was going to be slightly harder than I had thought. Maybe I should reduce my goals and go for a little bit every couple of days to get myself into some sort of reasonable state before I started going for the fitness regime.

Actually, as weedy as that sounded, it actually started to work and I started to reap the benefits. OK, I was never going to be an Olympic swimmer, or a marathon runner for that matter. Instead, my smaller, feebler attempts started to get me back on some sort of track. Before I knew it I was swimming forty lengths and still had enough energy to pat myself on the back when I got back to the changing rooms. My hair was still very short and the condensation from the pool made it curl up into tight curls. One member at the pool seemed to find this quite amusing, but after a hardened stare I really could not be bothered to tell him I was in recovery, so I chose to leave him and his ignorance alone.

By now, I was also out walking with friends, not over rough terrain, but padding around the streets at night, in the dark and cold, but chatting and laughing as we went, which meant you ended up walking farther than you originally intended. It may be a walk in the park for some of you reading this, but it got my heart pounding and I worked up a little bit of a gentle sweat, so that had to be good.

Preparation for travelling to the southern hemisphere also meant vaccinations. A timetable of needles was laid out, allowing enough time for preliminary shots to be followed by the boosters in readiness for my first flight out. With my recent history, I certainly wasn't shy of the needle and it came as welcome relief that I was being pumped full of antibodies for various diseases rather than the dreaded chemotherapy.

Plans I had just talked about started to fall into place. The charity had sent us a checklist and I was ticking more and more off. There was mention of wearing layers, both to keep warm and dry, and also to strip off as the temperature increased. I found myself having conversations about the benefits of walking poles, walking boots, breathable waterproofs, and sleeping bags which would cope with minus temperatures. It wasn't a simple case of packing a rucksack and throwing it on your back, the list ran into pages and pages with things I hadn't even considered like toilet rolls, head torch, dry shampoo. The charity provided a shopping voucher for an outdoor equipment retailer and, what I didn't have, I borrowed from Sarah who had walked the Inca Trail to Machu Picchu the year before.

Four weeks before the trip, in April, Sarah and Bruce took me to Ireland with the sole purpose of gaining trekking experience in the great outdoors. However, the true adventurer in me discovered Guinness again. It's like a healthy foodstuff, packed full of iron. Honestly! Sarah and I donned our numerous layers, special socks, boots, power bars and water bottles, topped the whole ensemble off with waterproofs, and set off with our map of the Ring of Kerry. Bruce took the opportunity to whizz off on his motorbike and enjoy the scenery as we set off in the horizontal wind and rain to complete our first adventure. After a few hours trying to keep upright was the first true test of outdoor life. I needed to pee. Darren had purchased the infamous "she-wee" for me and I hadn't yet plucked up courage to practice, so we stumbled into the trees and fern and discovered a quiet private spot to relieve ourselves. Sarah went first, to test the conditions and talked me through a step-by-step lesson on how to "do it" without getting it all over your trousers and into your boots. An age later, peace was resumed and liquid soap used, and we adjusted everything and set off again.

The next bit of our journey was like a stupid comedy movie. We assumed we were in the back of beyond, no human occupation for at least 20 miles, but, and you had to be there to appreciate it, around the corner sat a café. A big café in fact, with windows, a roof, menus, people and toilets. It was one of those moments we vowed never to talk of the incident again. Instead, we went in, had a big bowl of steaming soup and a big hot chocolate with cream on top, and then ended the whole ridiculous episode with a trip to the ladies toilet. This time for an indoor pee! Our walk included walking up a large hill, I can't say mountain, but it was a hill and it was big, to get to the top of a waterfall. The trek up was hard, but Sarah coached me all the way and I eventually made it, although, the source of the waterfall was a little disappointing, and it did cross my mind as I trudged and puffed and panted, that this business of walking up mountains may not be a lifelong passion of mine and Peru may be the only trek I do.

By May 2013, my training for the trek was going reasonably well, and my guest room had become Trek Peru Headquarters with everything I was due to carry now taking up the whole of the double bed and most of the floor. It took a couple of days to get it all into the pack I would have on my back and the bag that the porters would carry. We caught an early morning coach to the airport, where we met most of our team for the first time. We had a flight to Madrid and then picked up our long overnight flight to Lima wearing support socks and arm supports because post-cancer you are more at risk of DVT and lymphoedema. The next morning, hair all over the place, feeling tired and a bit grubby, we came out of Customs and we were in South America! It is everything you imagine, or have seen on TV. The noise, the people, the colours, the apparent chaos. We were then herded through to another departure lounge to wait for a smaller flight to Cusco to meet the remainder of the team and start our real adventure. We met some fabulous people and many have remained friends, all brought together by a sense of adventure, either cancer survivors themselves, or close to someone touched by it. Everyone had come for different reasons, from different circumstances, supporting a variety of charities, all with different stories. But we all had one goal, to reach the mystical city of Machu Picchu because we had been dealt a different card and we could.

I had long been fascinated by the mysteries surrounding Machu Picchu and had read lots of articles and books about it or watched lots of documentaries of the archaeological finds. I never truly thought I would make it there, but suddenly, within a few days I would be there. I was familiar with the history of how the Incas had been systematically wiped out by the Spanish conquistadors and their greed for gold.

The hotel in Cusco was clean, but basic and we were issued with our challenge t-shirts to provide photo opportunities along the way. We met our guides, who assured us they would be with us every step and stressed that the journey was NOT a race. It wasn't about who got there first, it was about safety and acclimatisation of the altitude and ensuring that everyone got there in one piece. They explained that you could walk at your own pace and that it was a team effort so everyone would stick together. I had never experienced altitude before and had felt its first effects soon after landing at Lima. Cusco lies even higher at over 11,000ft above sea level. You can feel that the air is thinner and you almost gulp in the air to try and get enough oxygen. You have a continual mild headache and feel slightly dizzy as you move around and the stay in Cusco is an attempt to allow your body to adjust. It affects people differently, and some felt quite poorly early on, some were oblivious to it, and for a change I was somewhere in between, and although I could feel it and it made me feel a bit odd, I certainly didn't feel ill.

We had about 24 hours before we set off on our first day and visited the Pikillaqta Ruins. Pikillaqta had been a city occupied by the Wari people and although people lived there, the city was used for ceremonies and feasting rituals. The Wari people were a short-lived empire, pre-dating the Incas by some 400 years and were wiped out long before the arrival of the Spanish, but their architecture and their art and pottery is similar to that of the Incas. What I hadn't realised before I went was that Machu Picchu is only one of many cities along the Inca Trail that had been abandoned and the trail acted as a long distance trade route between the cities.

The next day we were taken to the Lares Hot Springs. Lares has a history of ancient settlement but is currently lived in by people of Quechua descent, the indigenous population of South America, and Quechua is the language they speak. These are the people you will see on images of Peru who wear the brightly coloured jackets and hats, usually in red, children and adults alike. They are also the ones who are seen with alpacas, who also invariably have ribbons or garlands in their fleeces. I can tell you that an alpaca is smaller than a llama, produce high quality wool, can be seen scattered all over the hillside, just like our sheep, and they spit. Who said travel wasn't an education? So, there I was in the middle of Peru, rubbing shoulders with the descendants of the Inca, being spat at by an alpaca, and our guides and porters and chef set up, every mealtime, a tent with tables and tablecloths, chairs, flowers, cold drinks and gourmet style meals. I am a picky eater at the best of times, and had already decided before flying to Lima that I would not be tucking into the Peruvian speciality of roast guinea pig. Partly because I had a guinea pig as a childhood pet and had given him a name, Guin, but I had no problem eating anything else that was put before me, except anyone else's pet. How they produced the meals they did in the conditions they were working under, I have no idea, but the staff would produce three course meals which were tasty, nutritious and wonderful.

After a hearty lunch, we trekked even higher to Cuncani, which is set amongst harsh, high mountains. This was to be our spot for overnight, and when we arrived the porters had already set up our tents, the food tent and more importantly the toilet tents. This was no four star luxury, and a scarf over the nose and mouth always cut out the worst that nature could throw at you, but needs must. After you had done what was needed to be done over a hole dug in the ground, you almost had the Catholic ceremony of saying goodbye to it by sprinkling ash over it, walking away and not looking back!

So, the sky above me was pitch black with twinkling stars. They were so close I could almost have touched them. I was readjusting my layers in the dark as I stumbled back across rocks and dirt to my tent with only a head torch to guide me, when suddenly a random small child appeared from the side of the mountain. Needless to say she was less alarmed than I was. We had taken gifts of colouring pens, hair ties, balls, small toys, and I stumbled back to my tent to get some colouring pens. There was no verbal communication between myself and the child, but we had eye contact as I handed her the pens, and she took them from me and held onto them like they were the most precious thing on earth. Suddenly, another child appeared, then another. More gifts were handed out, the children said nothing but their faces said it all. They then scampered off into the darkness with their treasures. A simple touching moment that will stay with me forever.

Although I had camped a few times before, this experience was different, both funny and incredible. You sensibly kept most of your layers on in your sleeping bag, and if you were lucky, you would wriggle yourself into a position to pull the hood around your face so that only your nose was exposed. One night, we decided to treat ourselves and have a full body wash with wet wipes. This was NOT a good idea, we were frozen, the wet wipes were freezing and the tents weren't spacious with two fully grown women and two large rucksacks, boots, poles and other paraphernalia littered about so you were lucky if you didn't get an unknown body part stuck in your face. Lots of giggling, apologising, sharp intakes of breaths as the cold hit another bit of exposed skin, and if you listened carefully, our otherwise completely silent campsite was a series of tents of whispers, giggles and the flashing lights of the head torches.

After another hearty breakfast the next day we headed off on more trekking. Every now and again, being at the back due to my wheezing, the guide would stop me and tell me to take in the view. It was very easy to just keep leaning on your poles looking at your feet, avoiding alpaca poo, but this gave me the opportunity to stand and turn and see something I had never experienced before and probably never would again. We struck up quite a friendship walking for hours on end and he would talk to me about the Inca history, farming techniques, and the religious beliefs of the Quechua of the condor, the jaguar and the snake. Hmm, I knew about the condors, but sadly did not see any in flight, but none of the charity paperwork had mentioned getting bitten by a snake or eaten by a jaguar. And let's face it, I was the weakest of the pack and I was at the back…enough said. Mind that alpaca poo!

The following night it was arranged for the local children to come and visit us whilst their mothers would sell us their handmade wares. I bought some alpaca wool socks and a handbag. Well, you're on the side of a Peruvian mountain, what else does a girl buy but something for her feet and a bag? The children sat in a semi circle whilst we divided up the gifts and handed them out to them as they stared at us wide-eyed in their bright red traditional dress. We had visited a school previously and left some gifts and the joy of giving to such appreciative little faces was coupled with the joy of having reduced weight for our rucksacks. The children sang to us and then it was our turn to sing to them. *Twinkle Twinkle Little Star* was our preferred choice at the last minute which the children found hilarious for some reason.

Every morning, we were woken at 6am by the porters who gave us hot chocolate or coffee and a bowl of warm water for a wash. Then they would pack everything up and head off with laden horses to our next destination, sometimes running in flip flops up the mountain. Yes, running uphill in flip flops! The porters incidentally, not the horses!

Sadly, at this point I had not realised I had a problem with my Achilles tendon and I was compensating for this by leaning on one side as I trekked putting huge pressure on my hip. At one point, while I was wheezing, the doctor who was travelling with us and had been keeping a beady eye on me, wanted to take me off the trek as she said she could see me dragging my leg. At first

I flatly refused as I was determined to get to the top of this mountain. When I reached the summit, last as usual, with everyone sitting on rocks cheering me on, I broke down. The doctor walked over to me and hugged me and I remember looking over her shoulder at the incredible view of those huge mountains, oozing with power and history and knowing at that moment that I had reached my physical limit.

Despite everything, I was still in cancer recovery and was in terrible pain, but I knew I was looking at a once in a lifetime view that some who had, and still have cancer, would never see. But the mountains had beaten me, and I knew I had to head back down, I couldn't go on. The trek down should have been easier but the pressure on my ankles and knees was now becoming an issue as I stumbled down on broken rocks. The doctor offered me the chance of taking the journey on the back of one of the horses, but horses and me don't have a good relationship. Maybe that should have been another chapter in the book, but for the purpose of this trip, let's just say I preferred to stumble over the rocks and hurt my ankles.

We got back to camp and the doctor appeared with a nice big fat needle to inject an anti-inflammatory into my hip. Waaaaah that hurt, a lot! Later, as I lay in my tent, disappointed and in some discomfort, one of my fellow team-mates appeared and asked if she could perform some Reiki on us. I was prepared to give anything a go at that point, and I have to say, whether it was the Reiki, the shot from the doctor or that combined with the power of the mountains, I felt the pain ease.

The next morning the guide and doctor took me to one side and told me I was being taken off the trek. I'm afraid I experienced disappointment and relief in equal measure, because as much as

I knew I wanted to do this, I was worried I was doing untold damage to my recovering body. Another team-mate was also being taken off for other health reasons, so we were put on a truck and taken to the next trek meeting point. So, a truck, in South America, with a local driver, on a narrow mountain track with sheer drops on one side, says it all, because I think it is best I say no more about that experience. Put it this way, we survived it!

We were heading for a town called Ollantaytambo, which is another Inca city, with stepped terracing, ruins, and huge grain stores built precariously into the mountainside. We arrived long before the team, via the unmentionable hair-raising truck journey and found a café at the edge of the busy market where we ordered pizza, food from the gods, and an Inca Cola! Yes, the Incas had cola (they didn't, but it conjures up more mystery) and it's fizzy, and it comes in a glass bottle, and it's a bizarre fluorescent yellow. You expect cola, it says it quite clearly on the label, but as it hits your mouth another familiar flavour fills your taste buds. It's Irn Bru! Pizza and Irn Bru or walking up a mountain…you be the judge! I had died and gone to condor heaven! As we sat, dozing in the warm sunshine belching after a feast of fizzy drink and melted cheese, a dog walked past us in a summer Hawaiian style shirt and dungarees. Junk food hallucination? Nope, it was a dog in a shirt and dungarees. It really was! Burp!

We met up in the late afternoon with the team. The next morning we were getting the train to the Machu Picchu so that the team could get off a few stops early and see Machu Picchu from the Sun Gate. This is a gateway, high above the ridge of a mountain which looks down on the city and the place where the Incas, and now trekkers, would walk through and get their first view of the city. They were chatting about it excitedly on the train and I could feel the disappointment weighing me down that I couldn't see the city this way, but despite this, my own arrival, perhaps with less ceremony, was no less awe inspiring.

I was honoured to be there, amongst all the history, the mysticism that surrounds it, the people that lived there and walked the same tracks as I was, who walked through the doorways of the buildings I was standing in and who looked through the windows at the views I was now looking at, which had presumably changed very little over hundreds of years. You could feel the spirit of the place all over you. It twitched every pore of your body. I can't describe it very well. You sense the people are still there, standing next to you, behind you, around you, watching you. Not in a scary, ghost-like way, but their spirits and beliefs live on. I would stand silently just breathing it in. It's incredibly spiritual and peaceful. Quite a few of us felt very emotional. There was so much to take in. It's one of the most incredible places I had ever experienced. Absolutely incredible.

If you ever get the chance to go, don't think about it, just say yes. You don't have to do the trek to get there, you can get a train all the way from Ollantaytambo, but just seeing Peru is experience enough. The children were adorable, but the poverty is high and the life on the mountains is hard, which means families lose approximately a third of their children because of the conditions before they reach adulthood. When you meet the children they are funny, cheeky, polite, have big white-teeth smiles. They have very little by way of material things, and it doesn't seem to affect them, and when you give them a few pounds' worth of colouring pens or toys, they are beyond thrilled. Oddly, if it was not for breast cancer, I would never have experienced this wonderful country with its wonderful people and they would not had experienced me!

Well, the trip was over, I had seen things and experienced things I never would again. We flew out of Cusco, back to Lima, over the Equator and across the Atlantic to Madrid, then Heathrow. I was exhausted, happy and proud of what I'd achieved, because although I had been taken off the trek for medical reasons, I had only missed one day of trekking. I got home, with a huge pile of laundry, small token presents for everyone, some steroid weight loss because of course I had an infection while I was there. There were so many other things that had happened, that could easily fill a few more chapters, but this trip was about a personal journey for me. We had raised £13,000 for Breast Cancer Care and after all that I still hadn't seen Paddington Bear!

CHAPTER 25 – I'M BULLET PROOF

A couple of weeks following my return from Peru, my hip and left leg were stiff and still in severe pain. I returned to my GP and at the beginning of August 2013 I was referred back to oncology at Leicester Royal Infirmary. As usual, my breast area was checked for any change and with the new symptoms I was referred for an isotope bone scan. I had told the oncologist that a few months before, my GP had suspected the possibility of bone cancer. The oncologist was unsatisfied that only a blood test had been carried out to rule out this possibility and questioned why a scan had not been performed, given my recent medical history.

On the 12th August 2013 I was at Leicester for a nuclear

medicine bone whole body scan. The results had a quick turnaround thankfully, probably quicker than the time it takes to the read the full title of the scan and the results were clear. OK, I'm back on a roll! This same month, I was going for a hat-trick of cervical smear tests which I really needed to come back as normal to get back into my normal screening programme. By the beginning of October 2013 I had noticed a change in the scarring on my breast. This time my GP referred me back to Glenfield and after an ultrasound it was confirmed it was erosions on the scar tissue and nothing more. So, yet again, my results were clear. On 20th December 2013 I was back at Glenfield again for a check-up with my surgeon and my results were clear.

New Year and a new start in January 2014 I joined Slimming World and after toying with the diet and being good, then bad then good again, I managed to lose a stone in weight. Finally, I had said goodbye to the weight I had gained on my steroid diet. I was asked to do a talk at Slimming World about my diagnosis, my recovery, and my preparation for the Race For Life, which was coming up in the June. I was amazed as I found myself talking in front of approximately 50 women. It was my first brush with public speaking, and it went remarkably well, and little did I know it would not be my last.

For the first time in years I was getting clear results on all areas of my former worries, I had lost some weight, I was looking and feeling better and these weren't the only changes to my life. In February 2014, Darren and I decided, after seven years together to go our separate ways. After many hours talking it through and agonising over the decision we kept coming back to, we finally realised that we would never be able to reconcile the future of our relationship as we both wanted different things. It wasn't by any means the first time we had split up over the same thing, but this time I knew in my heart of hearts that this really was the last time. It was a difficult final decision to make over someone who had stood by me throughout my terrible journey, who had cared for me and supported me, physically and emotionally, who had shared my dark humour at my darkest times, but I knew he couldn't give me the life commitment I knew I both wanted and needed. We lived very much apart and there were no plans for us to have a future together. Sadly, the years are now just memories, but he was my personal and attentive carer throughout my illness and for this he will always remain an admired and valuable friend.

I was broken. My heart was broken and it would have been so easy to say "let's give it another try," but I knew that in weeks or months we would be back on the same merry-go-round of talking about wanting different things. I couldn't do it to him and I certainly couldn't do it to myself. I had come too far to start going backwards again. We had chosen our life paths and we needed to get on with our lives, and it wasn't to be together. By April 2014, I was still struggling with the fallout of the break up, so Sarah and Bruce packed me up, threw me in the car and insisted I go back to my Irish roots to drown some of my sorrows in more Guinness. Oh, all right then and off to Dublin we headed.

Sarah and I had already registered for the Race For Life 2014 in Bath and while we were waiting in the ferry car park to board the boat I had a call from the Press Department of Cancer Research asking me if I would like to represent Leicestershire. They had read my story that I had added on my application form and wondered if I would share it with others. I said yes, and then they asked if Sarah would represent Bath. How could we say no? They interviewed us over the phone and used a few quotes in both the *Leicester Mercury* and the *Bath Chronicle*, alongside a photograph I sent to them from when we took part in Race For Life before.

When I got home from Ireland I discovered that they had also passed my story to other press outlets and *The Sun* daily newspaper had picked it up. Not sure what I thought about that, other than, the more people that I could send the "check your breasts for signs of cancer" message, the better. *The Sun* called me and sent over a photographer and a make-up artist. All a little bit surreal to be honest but they asked if I could get Tom involved too. We had various shots taken of us at home, which were all a little bit excruciating, although the photographer was funny and kind and instantly put us at our ease. They had picked up on the Zumba angle, from where I had first noticed there was a problem, and the photographer had contacted me prior to arriving and asked if he could get some shots of me at a Zumba class. I cleared this with the ladies, who were all terribly keen, and we drove over to the class.

When I arrived, 60 women were all eagerly waiting for us and they were all dressed in pink. It was terribly funny and terribly emotional and they were all simply wonderful. But it became a real pity, and a hugely wasted opportunity, because the paper decided not to use the story. In many ways it was a complete waste of time, but we all enjoyed it anyway. My face and story continued to appear in local papers though, and I even had a brush with fame appearing in the *Daily Express* wearing my pink "Cancer, we're coming to get you!" t-shirt kindly provided by Cancer Research. A press company that send stories out to national magazines contacted me and tried to tempt me in with a cash reward. This really wasn't the route I wanted to go. It wasn't about the money, it was about getting the message of checking for early signs of cancer and how to deal with it. I had already experienced one of the newspapers getting some of the few simple basic facts wrong which had upset me as they featured me in a tiny report, so I didn't want to get into this. I refused and was met with astonishment over the phone.

After my brief and on the whole enjoyable brush with fame, on the 17th April 2014 I was referred back to Glenfield yet again as nodules had been detected on my scar tissue. Despite me insisting that it was scar tissue and that this was wasting everyone's time, the shadow of "Is it coming back?" sat over me in the waiting room again. A mammogram and ultrasound later confirmed that it was just scar tissue. Results – Clear.

I found myself single, spending time with Tom, building up my bookkeeping company again, eating healthily and still trying to lose some weight, keeping fit and active and balancing all this with looking after my dad who was slowly declining in health. Months were flying by and generally I was busy and happy, but there were moments, sitting on my settee at home, with a glass of wine in my hand watching the TV where I knew that I did not want to be alone for much longer. I needed to meet someone, I WANTED to meet someone. I am a natural carer and I did not have that "partner" to care for or them to care for me, so I am not at my best when I'm alone. Both Sarah and my neighbour kept telling me, in separate conservations, "Get yourself on the internet!" Oh no, had it really come to this? I had heard nothing from Gerard Butler, his phone must have been on silent, and the cat had eaten Peter Andre's roast!

So, one afternoon, when I came up with the excuse that it was too much money, Sarah pointed out that a one month subscription on the website was the same amount as a night out. Dammit, she was right, again. So I did it. I signed up. I filled in pages and pages of what I liked to eat, what I watched on TV, what I read, where I liked to go on holiday, what colour my sitting room carpet was…well OK that last one isn't true, but they may as well have asked because I spent an afternoon putting my entire life on a faceless computer and sat and waited for Gerard to call me. Well, he didn't, and after getting notifications from other profiles, a surprising amount I'm pleased to say, we're not talking "no response" at all here, just so you know, but when Jim from Derby had "sent me a smile" or Ed from Coventry or Steve from Lutterworth, I did hit the delete button a few times. Oh dear, sorry!

But just when you think all is lost, and you have extended your search criteria into East Anglia, up popped Michael from Norwich. OK, things were looking rosier. I'd always liked Norfolk and had taken many happy holidays there, so it's not the worst place to live. He didn't give the appearance of being a bunny boiler, and his profile seemed genuine and entertaining and he didn't appear to take himself too seriously. So, I sent a "smile" and I got a "smile" back. OK, things were hotting up in internet dating land! In no time at all we were exchanging questions and answers, which led to text messages and then phone calls.

After a short time, but many conversations later, we met in May 2014. I was not the slightest bit nervous as we knew everything about each other. The second I opened the door and he smiled and greeted me with a kiss on my cheek, I knew it was going to be OK. My neighbour and her husband had their supper resting on their window sill so they could keep an eye out, and Sarah and Tom would text me throughout the evening to say "Well?" and yes it all went very, very well. We talked early on about my breast cancer and he very openly talked about the recent loss of his second wife to motor neurone disease. There were no secrets from the start and that was important to me. We talked about my close relationship with Tom and we talked about his close relationship with his two sons, in their late teens, from his first marriage. It soon became apparent that we had both been through the trauma of illness, we were both alone and we both wanted a simple, happy, uncomplicated life that we could share. I'd found him and I had found love. Sorry, Gerard, I'm sure you're a nice chap, but you're too late.

In June 2014, Sarah and I, along with our "minder" Bruce, completed the Race For Life in Bath. It was a fabulous sunny day and we had the usual warm up with the local radio station. The DJ commented on the reasons we were all there and said if you had lost or come close to losing someone near to cancer, we were all there to make that change. Bruce put one arm around me and the other around Sarah, holding us tight. I was welling up but kept it together. Reality was hitting me again. As we "jogged," yes "jogged" around Victoria Park, Bruce was snapping photos as we went. Now and again we would take it back down to a fast walking pace as the wheezing was kicking in again. No change from 2012 then. This time we completed the course in 39.13 minutes. We were thrilled and we had raised £500 for Cancer Research and had a glass of fizz to celebrate. This time we even appeared on the Heart FM website front page!

Although the early stages of the relationship with Michael were long distance, we managed to find plenty of time to spend together, as his work takes him all over the country, so he could always manage a slight detour to the Midlands. Before I knew it, we were talking seriously about me moving to Norfolk and spending the rest of our lives together. We had both finally found what we were looking for, a true soul mate. I discussed it with Tom who was happy for me to go, but he didn't want to leave Hinckley. We decided to get him a flat, so I could stay with him and remain working in the town and still visit my dad, who could come out to Norfolk and get some good Norfolk air. At this point, I had undergone some of the Fostering training and passed the "Panel" with flying colours. I had been convinced that my cancer would be a massive "no." But quite the opposite actually. It classes me as having more life experience and I could relate to children going through a similar experience either themselves or a family member. As a matter of fact, quite a bit of my life experiences led to it being a definite yes, but I would have to re-apply if I was to move county, so this was not yet meant to be.

In the meantime, I was still having check-ups and on 22nd August 2014, I had an annual check-up with the breast care nurse. Results – Clear. My dad was still having his check-ups and scans too, which I could safely attend, but his health was deteriorating quite rapidly. He was losing weight at an unusually fast rate and I could see that the COPD was taking a firm grip of him. I could assess how well he was doing by our weekly supermarket shop, which was getting longer and longer and he walked around the store achingly slow. I also noticed he was doing less and less at home and taking less interest in things around him. He had met Michael a handful of times and seemed quite happy that I was getting on with life and moving to my new life in Norfolk, knowing of the plans for him to come out to visit, or better known as his holiday home!

I was spending some of my weekends in Norfolk and was meeting Michael's friends who were all welcoming and charming, as much to see Michael happy, as to meet me. One friend who tirelessly organises fundraising events called "She Is…" usually followed by the theme of the night, eg, "She Is Healthy." She was about to hold one of her events in Norwich in September and asked if I would tell my story. The evening was also being supported by the Keeping Abreast charity and I met one of the committee members who has become a good friend. Naturally, I jumped at the chance, and as I took my place on the stage in front of an audience of 220 it was not what I expected. There was silence. All you could hear was my voice, a little wobbly, but slowly and calmly I got through my story. I told the low parts as well as the funny parts, with people laughing in all the right places thankfully. I had captured their interest and hopefully they were able to take something from it. A resounding round of applause at the end finally broke the silence and I couldn't believe it! Afterwards I was asked to join the charity where I hope I can channel some of the fundraising skills and my life experience into this wonderful organisation.

Things were finally looking up for me and going my way, until, life had one more pop at me and threw tragedy in my path again. In November 2014, my dad was admitted to hospital with suspected kidney stones. After five scans and a week in hospital, it was revealed he had lung cancer and metastatic liver cancer. We had visited him daily but deep down we knew he was not going to come out of hospital. By chance on the Saturday I had requested to see a doctor as my dad was so unsettled, but none were available until the Monday morning. Day by day he was slowly going downhill and he would discuss his funeral arrangements with me. I would wash his face to make him feel better and try to make him laugh. I would take his washing home and desperately try to think of things he needed as he had lost all interest in everything. Even eating and swallowing water was a strain. I would stand in his empty flat, looking around for things to take, knowing it was unlikely he would return here. I had spent so long getting the local council to update his flat, new kitchen and a very recent new wet room as he could no longer lift his legs for the pain of the shrinking arteries and aneurysms.

By chance on the Monday, my mum, Tracey and I attended the hospital to see the doctor. I had brought my dad in some latte as he had enjoyed it the day before, but sadly he never got to drink it. It was as though every ten minutes he was getting worse. I requested morphine from the ward sister who gratefully administered this and it calmed him. He took my hand and placed it on his abdomen and whispered, "Hot." I had agreed with him but to me it did not feel hot. For the last time I washed his face. I asked him if it was nice and he frailly nodded. This was to be our last conversation and deep down through the tears I knew. The doctor arrived at his bedside and the diagnosis was finally given, along with only 24 hours to live and the need to get the "End of Life Team" to attend to him. At this declaration my dad took his last breath. We had no time to get the end of life team. He saved them all the bother. I was there with him, stroking his head and holding his hand. Although I had come to terms that it was unlikely he would leave hospital again, the end was still a shock. It's very, very sad to see a close loved one die from lung cancer. From the years of smoking, the last breaths are strained and you pray for it to be soon.

I had never had a really close relationship with my dad, until the last six years of caring for him. My relationship with him had changed to one of a sort of understanding that I was there for him whatever happened and he knew it. It was a bit like a marriage. I would take him homemade cakes and dinners, clean for him and laugh at some of the funny things the "older" generation would say, like getting things totally wrong and you subtly having to correct them. I promised him I would care for Tom who had visited a couple of days before, but deep down Tom knew this would be the last visit too. We had a concern that my dad was not requesting morphine, you know, to not put anyone to any trouble so his only grandson spoke up for him. This was Tom's first bereavement and something we are still coming to terms with. It is odd losing a parent as it's a person you have known your entire life. He is very sadly missed. He was named after King George VI and his mother had been presented with a scroll and a mug from the King, possibly for her contribution of the population in Rutherglen but these were put into the local library for safekeeping. My dad recalled seeing them as a child on school visits as the other children would point in awe at him and the personal relics. Sadly, after 15 years of trying to retrieve them for him they cannot be located. He had enjoyed the parts of my book that he had read, exclaiming "It's very good!" He never made much of a fuss over anything but I think it is!

Suddenly, I had bereavement, two house moves (mine and Tom's), a flat to clear, funeral arrangements to organise and a will to sort out, as my dad had made me sole executor. Not much time to sit around then. With my usual panache and organisational skills I did it, all of it surviving on four hours sleep a night over the two weeks. I read the tribute at his funeral. I finally said goodbye to "Monkey", my nickname for him, and gave my last gift to him of a bagpiper playing at the crematorium. Cancer had hit us one more time, but this time it had taken my dad. Was it ever going to leave me alone?

At this stage I was being tested for a suspected fibroid caused probably by Tamoxifen. After a scan and biopsy I had the results in January 2015. It was confirmed to not be cervical cancer or secondary cancer, though I didn't know they were testing for these and I am very grateful that I was not told. It was decided that it was to be left alone. No surgery. No hysterectomy. No cancer. I will remain on tablets for it and hopefully, in two years' time when I should hit menopause full on it will start to shrink. Heck, more hot sweats then!

My fundraising continues and cancer has now become a large part of my life, with a determined will to continue to beat it. Over the last three years, I have been part of various teams that have raised over £50,000 for cancer charities – Breast Cancer Care, Breast Cancer Campaign, Cancer Research and donations made to Macmillan Cancer Support, Coping with Cancer, Headstrong and LOROS, which was my local cancer hospice. I have taken part in two Race For Life events, and a muddy one is in the diary for summer 2015. The week my dad passed away, my neighbour and I held a charity night for Cancer Research at a local pub. My dad knew of this arrangement and the loss of him gave me a bigger reason to go round the pub taking donations for such a worthy cause. A friend of mine works for Neal's Yard and through an evening of a beauty demonstration we raised £420, which was in addition to another Neal's Yard evening, organised by another friend, where six of us raised £60. I have also signed up to the Breast Cancer Care Lottery. It's not quite as big as THE National Lottery, but I've managed to win twice, which is always nice.

So as I near the end of this particular story, where am I now? You've stuck with me all this time, you've read all my highs, my lows, my personal bits, the sad bits, the happy bits, the ridiculous bits so the least I can do is give you a happy ending. Well, that's partly down to Michael. I had made a Wish List when I was first diagnosed and I am happy to say that over half of it has been achieved. My wishes included Tom being successful in life and love, that I lived out my days with a man who truly loved me and to live happily ever after in a cottage. Think positive always and you will be amazed as to what can happen.

I am now living my dream in a cottage in Norfolk. I have old latches on my doors, I have a real fire in a large fireplace, I have low doorways, outbuildings, a gravel driveway, I have the biggest garden that sweeps down to fields, my cats, all four of them (yes gained another three), are running around the garden and I have Michael. He has changed my life and made me happier than I have ever been. We have both been through the hardest of times, so now we embrace life and live it. We have nights out, nights in, we go away for weekends, we've been on warm tropical holidays, we like walks on the beach in Norfolk with the wind whipping up the sea with hot chocolate for afters. But most of all, we have both found true love and this will be the bond that keeps us strong and together. I can't bear any more loss.

And me? Who have I become? Before I know it, and certainly not overnight, I have become someone I would have barely recognised a few years ago. I am a stronger, confident woman, healthier than I have been in years, with a sure sense of purpose. I know what I want and I am not going to be held back when I have set my mind on something. I am determined to get out of life as much as I put in and I am not going to wait for opportunities to come knocking, I am going to go out and find them. Life throws all sorts of rubbish in your way, but you just have to get through it and get on with it. I can see things for what they are now and how precious life is and how easily it can be taken from you. I will stay under the radar of annual mammograms until I am 50 and know that I am in the safest of safe hands.

I haven't forgotten or forgiven cancer, how can I? It's left me, hopefully for good, but I know that I will continue to have brushes with it. I think I have said it before, but I know the war isn't over. I have won my own battle, and for the moment I will pat myself on the back for that. Taking a positive from cancer, which isn't easy, is that it has taught me all of this. If it hadn't visited me, uninvited, what would I be doing? Who knows? I'm not wiser, not by a long stretch, but I will quietly thank cancer for giving me the opportunity of seeing life from the other side, nearly, and for giving me the strength and positive outlook on life to know that I wanted to stay here, but that's all I will ever thank it for. If you're reading this, and you're in the midst of treatment, you have to remain strong and positive, you just have to, because please remember, tomorrow you will feel a little bit better, and the next day and the next. If you are a carer or part of a support team, your role is immense. You should be proud of yourself. If you haven't experienced cancer, just check yourself, please just check regularly. Don't find yourself on this journey, because it's not easy and it's not just breast cancer, it's *all* cancers. It can choose anywhere and it can choose anyone and it takes all around you with it, that I do know. But it's down to you, and one body and one mind to beat it. Make yourself bullet-proof!

EPILOGUE – TOM'S VERDICT

Before my mum was diagnosed with breast cancer, we had had trouble before with various potential illnesses. I remember being comforted by family at this point saying that whatever it was, she would make it through. I had never had a family member, especially this close, to be diagnosed with such a dangerous illness.

I remember the day she came back from the hospital with the diagnosis results. I rushed downstairs, prepared for the worst. When she told me, I knew that straight away it was something that could be dealt with. From day one I was convinced that she'd make it through unscathed and that it was just a challenge that God had put before us. Obviously she was upset, but I think even she knew that deep down she would beat it.

The day of her first operation was probably the longest in recent memory. I had gone to stay with my aunty for a couple of days and I was constantly thinking, "She'll be going down to theatre in 10 minutes," and such like.

From then on, I was fairly sensitive about the subject. A few of my friends knew what was happening at home, and my teachers were really supportive. It was not something I was embarrassed about, as it was something beyond my control, but people would be tense around me and try their hardest not to mention the "C" word.

It's such an awful thing to say but I never once visited my mum in hospital. I'd always seen her as this healthy, funny best friend and did not want to see her hooked up to machines and struggling to stay awake with no colour in her face. Luckily Darren was there to take her to and from the hospital as I could not drive at that point, and God forbid would it be left to me to shower her!

Thankfully, my mum did beat it, and it was a huge weight lifted when I heard the news that she had the all-clear, along with the six month check-ups later repeating the same sentence.

I feel very lucky to have my mum still around as some people are not as lucky, and we know now that if she can beat a life-threatening illness, she can get through anything.

Tom

MY ONGOING AFTER EFFECTS FROM CANCER

I said I would take the consequences, but who cares, I'm still here!

"Chemo hand" – I feel a restricted grip or it tires easily when writing for too long.

"Chemo brain" - Says it all really for those who know me!

Left breast – Still a bit numb but it didn't kill me!

Blood pressure and bloods – Cannot be taken from left arm due to lymph node removal.

Avoiding lymphoedema in my left arm – To avoid infection, kettle or iron steam, insect bites, scratches, punctures as in needles for blood tests, holding or carrying heavy items, leaning or putting pressure on the arm, holding hot items in my hand.

Tamoxifen – Breast cancer preventative tablet to be taken daily for five years which has caused a fibroid, so another tablet is taken for this too.

Levothyroxine – Another daily tablet for thyroid so my body functions normally.

Nasal passages – These can burn and a cold adversely affects my adenoids.

Mints – I can't eat strong mints either as they are too painful for the burning sensation.

Radiotherapy lung damage – The wheezing continues but I get by. I can swim like an athlete now but I think my mountaineering days are over!

Radiotherapy tiredness – Any excuse, as it comes over me suddenly and I go very pale but I constantly fight it. I look like I've had a shot of chemo!

Pain in my right foot – Tenderness from the anaesthetic from my second surgery.

Weak nails – They snap easily, so I have to keep them short and preferably painted for added strength.

Teeth – Slight discolouring from chemotherapy but regular check-ups help.

Sunburn – I can't, but then no-one should. The sun is a benefit but use sun cream always!

Eating slower than normal – Don't know why unless it's crisps!

Hair "down below" – still don't know what's going on down there but then I'm not sure I ever did! It's still patchy after chemotherapy.

It must be Having A Bad Hair Day!

THANK YOU IS NEVER ENOUGH

Tom - My wonderful son for stroking my baldy head and letting me live my life.

Darren – My very own private nurse and remaining an invaluable friend forever.

Sarah – Ongoing support and editing my book (bad language removed! Damn it!)

Bruce – His everlasting support, who has always been more than a brother-in-law.

Tracey – Holding it together for biopsy results and my first chemotherapy session.

My parents – Continued life support until the disease took my dad.

My extended family – For their love, care and support.

My best friend and her mum – Their support through thick and thin, like always.

My Peru buddy – Unlimited help and guidance from her breast cancer experience.

Friends and neighbours – Ongoing support for all of us.

Tom's school and friends – For helping Tom through his most difficult time.

My clients – Sticking with me and letting me work when I was well enough.

Business colleagues – For bearing with my Chemo Brain!

Additional support network – For the well-wishers who were unknown to me.

Cats – Louis, Clawdia, Scaredy, Muttley and Yogi - Past and present, being the entertainers they are and their unconditional love.

MDT – Getting it spot on. Thank you so much for my life.

My GP – Referring me and the squatter to Glenfield early on.

Breast Care Centre, Glenfield Hospital, All staff – For their breast cancer care and support for Trek Peru.

Breast care nurses – Being available 24/7 with their love and everlasting care.

Angel In Scrubs – Evicting the squatter first time round and for being an angel.

Hero In Scrubs – Timeless care and perfect surgery. Thank you will never say enough.

Knight Of Oncology – His care and advice on chemotherapy and radiotherapy. He is a true gentleman.

Surgery Pre-Assessment Team, Glenfield Hospital – Taking the time to ask how I felt and preparing me for surgery.

Radiation Team, Glenfield Hospital – Making pre-surgery as pain free as possible.

Theatre Team, Glenfield Hospital – Tucking me into bed after surgery with drugs!

Chemotherapy Team, Leicester Royal Infirmary – Looking after my shaking bones!

Phlebotomists – Taking the blood from a non-existent vein.

Radiotherapy Team, Leicester Royal Infirmary – Giving me the strength to finish.

Bone Cancer Scan Team, Leicester Royal Infirmary – For their kind assistance and stopping me from panicking!

Headstrong – Teaching me about headwear, care of my scalp and cups of tea!

Look Good, Feel Better – Giving me my features back and lots of scrummy goodies.

Coping With Cancer – A Counselling service that cannot be replaced.

Breast Cancer Care – Booklet Support – Peace of mind and teaching me everything.

Breast Cancer Campaign – Fundraising support for the cranberry cakes.

Daily Express – Printing my feature on breast cancer awareness.

Hinckley Times - Printing my feature on breast cancer awareness.

Leicester Mercury - Printing my feature on breast cancer awareness.

Bath Chronicle - Printing my feature on breast cancer awareness.

Heart FM – Sticking Sarah, Bruce and I on the front page!

Hairdressers – Cutting my long hair to a bob pre-chemotherapy treatment and giving me the tiniest haircuts in the world now.

Slimming World – Assisting in the loss of the steroid weight.

Zumba Team – Support on my return and for the newspaper features.

Charity Challenge – Trek Peru – To new and remaining friends for all their support and getting me to Machu Picchu.

Cancer Research UK – Race for Life Representative and ongoing fundraising.

MacMillan Cancer Support – Advice on finances.

LOROS (Leicester Hospice Charity) – For the service you provide. I knew you were there in case I needed you. I didn't, so I donated instead.

"She Is" – Giving me the strength for public speaking at the "She Is" event and the chance to tell my story and hopefully guide others.

Keeping Abreast Reconstruction Support Group – Their support to breast cancer patients in Norfolk.

Steven Ho and Pan Pantziarka – For converting my manuscript into a published eBook and paperback.

Jenny Ng – Her excellent work in the final proofread and edit.

Neil Davison – My Illustrator for his perfect book cover illustrations.

Imogen Davison – My Graphic Designer for her artistic skills.

All these people were involved in one person's journey.

And last, but by no means, to **Michael** – For letting me live the dream x

Printed in Great Britain
by Amazon